eXplore

Bible notes for adults

KT-226-370

October – December 2011

In this issue

The 92 daily readings in this issue of *Explore* are designed to help you understand and apply the Bible as you read it daily. Sections in this edition include readings from 1 Thessalonians, Daniel, 1 Timothy, Ecclesiastes and Luke.

It's serious!

We suggest that you allow 15 minutes each day to work through the Bible passage with the notes. It should be a meal, not a snack! Readings from other parts of the Bible can throw valuable light on the study passage. These cross-references can be skipped if you are already feeling full up, but will expand your grasp of the Bible.

Sometimes a prayer box will encourage you to stop and pray through the lessons—but it is always important to allow time to pray for God's Spirit to bring His word to life, and to shape the way we think and live through it.

We're serious!

All of us who work on *Explore* share a passion for getting the Bible into people's lives. We fiercely hold to the Bible as God's word—to honour and follow, not to explain away.

Contributors to this issue
- Graham Beynon • Carl Laferton •
- John Richardson •
- Tim Thornborough • Mark Wallace •

For information on how to subscribe, and our other Bible-teaching and training materials, please visit:

UK & Europe: www.thegoodbook.co.uk
N America: www.thegoodbook.com
Australia: www.thegoodbook.com.au
New Zealand: www.thegoodbook.co.nz

or contact us at admin@thegoodbook.co.uk

How to use Explore

Find a time you can read the Bible each day

Find a place where you can be quiet and think

Ask God to help you understand

Carefully read through the Bible passage for today

Study the verses with *Explore*, taking time to think

Pray about what you have read

the**goodbook**
COMPANY

Welcome to Explore—a resource to help you dig into, understand and apply the timeless truth of God's word to your life.

It can be a struggle to find a daily time to spend with God. Children, the busyness of life, special nights out, holidays, or just sheer exhaustion can all conspire to get in the way. However, there is no substitute for just getting into a good habit. There are many patterns that suit different people, and yours may change over time.

Whatever you choose to do, guard your time with God jealously. If you come hungry to learn from the Lord, and to feed on the truth, it will be a place of nurture and growth, and a source of direction and strength for your daily life.

◗ TIME: Find a time when you will not be disturbed, and when the cobwebs are cleared from your mind. Many people have found that the morning is the best time, as it sets you up for the day. You may not be a "morning person" so last thing at night, or, if you're free, a mid-morning break suits others. Whatever works for you is right for you.

◗ PLACE: Jesus says that we are not to make a great show of our religion (see Matthew 6 v 5-6), but rather pray with the door to our room shut. So, any-where you can be quiet and private is the key. Some people plan to get to work a few minutes earlier and get their Bible out in an office, or some other quiet corner.

◗ PRAYER: Although *Explore* helps with specific prayer ideas from the passage, you should try to develop your own lists to pray through. Use the flap inside the back cover to help with this.

Often our problem is not so much *who* to pray for, as *what to pray for them*! That's why Bible reading and prayer are inseparable. We are reminded from God's word of what is truly important; it will shape what we pray for ourselves, the world and others.

◗ SHARE: As the saying goes: *expression deepens impression*. So try to cultivate the habit of sharing with others what you have learned. It will encourage both them and you. Using the same notes as a friend will help you encourage each other to keep going.

REMEMBER:
- **IT'S QUALITY, NOT QUANTITY, THAT COUNTS:** *Better to think briefly about a single verse, than to skim through pages without absorbing anything.*
- **FALLING BEHIND:** *It's inevitable that you will occasionally miss a day. Don't be paralysed by guilt. Just start again.*
- **IT'S ABOUT DEVELOPING A LOVE RELATIONSHIP, NOT A LAW RELATIONSHIP** *Don't think that "doing your quiet time" is an end in itself. The sign that your daily time with God is real is when you start to love Him more and serve Him more wholeheartedly.*

Tim Thornborough, *Explore Editor*

By the rivers of Babylon

A re you ready for a rollercoaster ride? You'll need to be!

▶ **Read Psalm 137**

If you managed to read it without whistling the version by the group *Boney M*, you did well. If you managed to read it without taking a sharp intake of breath at the last two verses, you did even better. Lots of Christians have stumbled over the violent passion of this psalm. It is anti-Christian, some say. It is sub-Christian say others. It is neither says *Explore*! You only have to read **Luke 19 v 44** to get the clue. Yes, Jesus Himself quotes it!

Longing for home?

▶ **Read v 1-3**

They wept out of much more than home-sickness. Remembering Jerusalem brought to mind their shame and dishonour. The destruction of Jerusalem and their exile were all part of God's judgment on His unfaithful people. And more. There are signs in this psalm that the purpose of that judgment is being fulfilled. There is grieving too for the shame and dishonour that their waywardness brought upon God's name.

> *time out*
> ❓ *Have you ever crashed as a Christian?*
> Restoring a failed Christian takes more than sorrow over what has been done. It is easier to regret the harm that sin does to ourselves and others than it is to

> *time out*
> acknowledge how deeply it wounds our God, and how greatly He is shamed in front of the world by our faithlessness.

My highest joy

▶ **Read v 4-6**

It's easy to forget. The exiles can rise above slavery (Daniel, Esther). The land is far away, and not without it charms: river and trees. But the psalmist pronounces a curse upon himself: struck dumb and skills lost if he does not remember that Jerusalem is his highest joy.

> *time out*
> Us too. Heaven seems so remote. The world is not without its joys and toys, beauty and distractions. But we are cursed if we forget where home really is.
> **Read Matthew 6 v 19-21**

My deepest longing

▶ **Read v 7-9**

This is not personal vindictiveness. After all, the psalmist is only quoting back to God what He has promised elsewhere: namely to judge those who oppress His people. Not just this generation but in the future as well. If the sentiment seems shocking to us, then perhaps we need to re-awaken ourselves to how serious the wrath of God is against those who oppose Him. The anguish they would feel at the death of their children is just retribution for the anguish they have caused to God's people.

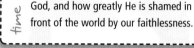

1 Thessalonians

❓ *How would you describe your Christian life today?*

A blessed church

▶ **Read 1 Thessalonians 1 v 1**

The church of the Thessalonians was in two places. Geographically, it was in Thessalonica (modern-day Greece, on the Aegean coast). But it was also "in God the Father and the Lord Jesus Christ".

❓ *How could this be so?*

❓ *"Grace and peace to you" was a normal way to begin a letter in those days. But what do you think Paul meant by this sentence as he began his letter?*

> time out
>
> It is easy for Christians to take grace and peace for granted. Don't! Take a few moments to think: what would your life be like without God's grace and God's peace? Now give thanks to God!

A blossoming church

▶ **Read v 2-3**

❓ *Why is Paul so thankful?*

❓ *Why is thanking God an appropriate response to the behaviour of the Thessalonians?*

❓ *Can you name ten people at your church who are showing these signs of faithful Christian living? Write their names down, and briefly give thanks to God for each one...*

Faithful Christians	
1.	6.
2.	7.
3.	8.
4.	9.
5.	10.

Faith, love and hope (v 3) are often grouped together in Paul's writings. We will see all three again in 5 v 8. *Faith* is trusting in God, and believing His wonderful promises. *Love* is putting God and other people first, seeking to serve him and them rather than ourselves. *Hope* is being confident that Christ is King, and our future with Him is secure. All three are gifts from God—it is only by His grace that we can be filled with true faith, true love and true hope. But once He has filled us in this way, faith and love and hope will start to affect how we think and act...

❓ *Why does faith produce work?*

❓ *Why does love prompt labour?*

❓ *Why does hope inspire endurance?*

> apply
>
> Our Christian faith, love and hope should influence every area of our lives.
>
> ❓ *How is this true for you?*
>
> ❓ *What things do you need God's help to work on?*
>
> Talk to God now about your answers.

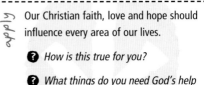

Imitating, and being imitated

3

▶ **Reading:** 1 Thessalonians 1 v 4-7

Monday 3 October

*R*ole models are very influential. Good ones are great. Bad ones can be disastrous. This is true in any area of life, but especially so in the Christian life. Modelling ourselves on older, wiser Christians is a great way to grow in the faith. And we can in turn become good role models for others. As the Thessalonians were finding...

▶ **Read 1 Thessalonians 1 v 4-7**

❓ What was it about the Thessalonians that had been helpful for the believers in Macedonia and Achaia?

❓ How would the Thessalonians have learned this from the lives of Paul and Jesus?

apply

❓ Which three people have most influenced you in your Christian life so far?

❓ How have you imitated them?

Take time to talk to God about these people now.

time out

Turn to **1 Corinthians 10 v 31 – 11 v 1** and ask yourself:

❓ What is it about Paul's example that is good to follow?

❓ How might his example affect the way you speak and act:

• with your family and relatives?

• with your non-Christian friends?

• with your church family?

Welcoming the message...

❓ How had the Thessalonians' response to the gospel proved the sincerity of their faith?

When the gospel comes to God's chosen people, it comes with more than just words. It comes with such power and conviction—through the Holy Spirit—that it changes people.

apply

❓ How have you personally experienced the Holy Spirit's powerfully convicting work?

❓ Are you modelling a godly response to the gospel message? How?

...in spite of severe suffering

We can't be sure exactly what form the suffering of v 6 took, but it was clearly severe. 2 v 14 and **Acts 17 v 5-9** suggest that it is likely to have been at the hands of their fellow Thessalonians—because of their allegiance to King Jesus.

❓ How is joy in the face of suffering possible for a Christian?

❓ What difference does the gospel make for you when you're suffering?

❓ Are you a role model in this area?

pray thru'

Pray for those Christians you know who might be influenced by you.

Pray that you might be a helpful role model for them.

BIBLE IN A YEAR: **EZEKIEL 33-34** • **JOHN 16**

The difference church makes

I live close to some church bells. When they ring out, we all know about it. Up close, they can be deafening.

Something else was ringing out from Thessalonica. What was it?

▶ **Read 1 Thessalonians 1 v 8-10**

❓ *How had their faith in God become known everywhere?*

It can be easy to over-complicate the Christian life. But at its heart, it's really very simple. We **turn**. We **serve**. We **wait**. Just like the Thessalonians, and just like all other Christians throughout the ages. It's not easy. But this turning and serving and waiting can have a profound effect on those around us, just like it did for the Thessalonians back then.

Turning

❓ *What had the Thessalonians turned from and to?*

❓ *Why would this turning have been so noticeable?*

> *apply*
>
> Our idols may be different from theirs, but no less dangerous.
>
> ❓ *What idols have you turned from? And what idols do you struggle with? List them:*
>
> And pray about them.

Serving

The Thessalonians had been serving idols—idols that were dead and false. But not now.

❓ *What will it mean for you to be serving the living and true God?*

Waiting

Remember their "endurance inspired by hope in our Lord Jesus Christ" (v 3).

❓ *When do you find it hardest to endure as a Christian?*

❓ *How might this verse help you at such times?*

> *time out*
>
> The coming wrath will be terrible. Read the account of it in **2 Thessalonians 1 v 6-10**. How easy it is to overlook this. How horrible to have to dwell on it. But how essential it is that we are rescued from it...

Turning. Serving. Waiting. See how all three go together. But some try to serve without having turned. Others are waiting, but not too bothered about serving. Which of the three do you find hardest?

Talk to God about it now, and ask for His help.

> *pray thru'*
>
> Pray for your church—that its faith in God may become known everywhere.

God's work, God's way

❓ *Was Paul a failure?*

He must have looked like one! Opposed, insulted, persecuted—and eventually kicked out of town. His ministry looks like a failure. And wouldn't that make Paul himself a failure too?

Not so, says Paul.

▶ **Read 1 Thessalonians 2 v 1-4**

❓ *How had Paul proved that he was worthy to be entrusted with the gospel?*

❓ *How would Paul define "success" and "failure"?*

Presumably, Paul could have been popular. He could have said what people wanted to hear. He was clever, so misleading people wouldn't have been difficult. If he had wanted to please people, he could have done so.

❓ *But pleasing people isn't the point. What is the point? (v 4)*

> *apply*
>
> ❓ *Can you join with Paul in saying verse 4 with integrity?*
>
> Pray about your answer.

▶ **Read v 5-12**

❓ *What did God-pleasing ministry involve for Paul?*

❓ *How would you summarise all the ideas into one sentence?*

Notice that Paul says he was like both a mother and a father. He was gentle, like a mother caring for her children (v 7)—loving, sharing and working hard (v 8-9). He also encouraged, comforted and urged the believers to live lives worthy of God, just like a father with his children.

❓ *Think for a moment of how you live your life around other Christians. How could you be more Paul-like (and Christ-like)?*

> *time out*
>
> Think of the leaders of your own church.
>
> ❓ *What does it mean for them to be like a mother and like a father for your church?*
>
> ❓ *What do you think they are finding difficult at the moment?*
>
> ❓ *What encouragement do you think they need this week?*
>
> Take time out to pray for them right now.

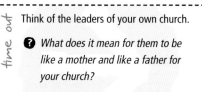

Living to please God

I n 2 v 1-12, we thought about a **ministry** that pleases God. Here, we're going to think about a **response** that pleases God.

Remember how the Thessalonians have been serving as a model to other believers (1 v 6-7)—welcoming the gospel with joy in spite of suffering? Well, here's more of the same.

Accepting...

▶ **Read 1 Thessalonians 2 v 13**

❓ What had the Thessalonians properly understood?

❓ Have you understood this too? What proof is there that you have responded to the gospel not as the word of men, but as the word of God?

❓ Can you list five ways in which the word of God is at work in you? Talk to God about them now.

The word of God is at work by...

1.

2.

3.

4.

5.

...while suffering

▶ **Read v 14-16**

❓ What have the Thessalonians had in common with other churches in Judea?

Has anyone ever told you that following Christ will make life nice and easy? If they have, they were lying. The Thessalonians suffered. As did Paul. So did other churches at the time. So did Jesus and the prophets. In fact—wait for it—*"everyone who wants to live a godly life in Christ Jesus will be persecuted, while evil men and imposters will go from bad to worse, deceiving and being deceived"* (2 Timothy 3 v 12-13).

❓ What ideas are there in 1 Thessalonians 2 v 13-16 to encourage us as we suffer?

> *time out*
>
> **Read Philippians 1 v 27-30.**
>
> ❓ What strategies does Paul commend when Christians are opposed?
>
> Think of those you know enduring such suffering at the moment, and pray for them by name.

Some would argue that 2 v 14-16 proves Paul was anti-semitic. Passages like **Romans 9 – 11**, however, show this cannot be the case. Ultimately, Paul is acutely conscious of God's wrath towards those who reject Christ and oppose Christ's people. To what extent does the wrath of God affect your everyday thinking? Pray now for those you know who are hostile to the gospel message and its messengers.

Timothy's task

Reading: 1 Thessalonians 2 v 17 – 3 v 5

Think back to the opening of the letter. Remember the phrase *"your labour prompted by love"* in 1 v 3? Well, let's see today how our love for others matches Paul's love for others...

An intense longing

Read 1 Thessalonians 2 v 17-20

? What words or phrases show Paul's depth of feeling?

? From what we have already seen in the letter, does the strength of Paul's emotions surprise you?

pray thru'

It would seem that most churches today lack this intensity of loving relationship.

? Why do you think this is?

Take time to talk to God about your church now.

? Why is the gospel of Christ the best way of strengthening and encouraging those undergoing trials?

apply

? Can you think of times in which your faith might come attack?

? How will the gospel of Christ help you at such times?

time out

? How aware are you of how other Christians are growing in the faith?

? Would you necessarily notice if they were unsettled or struggling?

Talk to God about your answers.

A godly concern

Read 1 Thessalonians 3 v 1-5

It would seem that the Thessalonians were in danger of being unsettled by their trials (v 3) and tempted by the devil (v 5).

? Why do you think Paul was fearful (v 5) that his efforts might have been useless?

? What was to be Timothy's task?

Now we really live

E ver had that experience of waiting for important news? Of waiting for the postman to arrive? Of the nervous anticipation—will it be good news, or bad?

Paul must have experienced something similar. He had heard of the Thessalonians' struggle. He was fearful for their well-being. And so he had sent Timothy to help them, and was now waiting to hear back. What sort of news would Timothy bring?

time out

Remember that their faith was held up as an example to others. And yet they still have far to go. Commenting on this passage, Calvin says: "Hence, whatever progress we may have made, let us always keep in view our deficiencies, that we may not be reluctant to aim at something higher".

❓ *However strong your faith, how might you aim at something higher?*

Good news

▶ **Read 1 Thessalonians 3 v 6-10**

❓ *How would you describe Paul's reaction to the news he receives?*

❓ *What, specifically, is Paul delighted about:*

   in v 6a?

   in v 6b?

   in v 7?

   in v 8?

❓ *Do we readily share Paul's joy, when we too hear of other Christians standing firm? Why, or why not?*

time out

And yet... all is not yet finished! Paul is aware that something is lacking in their faith (v 10), and so he still longs to see them again—presumably so that he can teach and correct them.

Great prayers

▶ **Read v 11-13**

It was probably five years before Paul got to see the Thessalonians again (**see Acts 20 v 1-3**). Presumably he kept praying these prayers for a long time.

❓ *What are Paul's priorities in his prayers?*

pray thru

❓ *How could you turn these verses into a prayer for those in your church?*

Spend time praying in these verses now.

Facing the future

What will the next weeks, months, years bring? Joy and success... or disaster and ruin? David gives us an object lesson in how to face the future when you're living in a foreign land.

▶ **Read Psalm 138**

Praise among the idols

▶ **Read v 1-2**

Even though David is far away, and surrounded by "gods", there's only one God that he will be serving—the true and living God. Even though he is surrounded by pagan temples, and enticing sights, David still remembers Jerusalem (v 2), and as a symbol of that turns in the right direction when he prays. Notice how unstinting his commitment is: "with all my heart" (v 1). David would have rebuked someone who said to him: "Let's have a time of worship". His reply might well have been: "No brother, let's have a *life* of worship!"

God's glory—my chief concern

▶ **Read v 2-3**

God had "exalted above all things His name and word". In other words, God's character and reputation (as a faithful, caring, promise-keeping God) are what really matter. That is what David is upholding as, with bated breath, he bows, not towards the statues of pagan gods, but towards the dwelling place of the almighty.

time out

Even though he lives among idol worshippers, David, dangerously, shows contempt for them. We too are surrounded by those who worship power, influence, worldly wisdom, family, children, money, good looks and talent. They will be shocked when we suggest that these things are unworthy of worship. Verse 3 tells us how to arm ourselves for the inevitable backlash...

My protection—God's chief concern

▶ **Read v 6-8**

But we've not been plonked into the lions' den and left alone. Notice:

• God watches over us (v 6)

• God preserves our lives (v 7)

• God's purposes will be fulfilled in us (v 8)

So we face the future with not the slightest shred of uncertainty about our ultimate destiny (that's the new creation), and with clear marching orders (to bring praise to God's name and word). All that is required is that we actually do it...

pray thru'

Pray through the words of this psalm, committing yourself to God whatever the future may bring.

Living God's will for our lives

Most people resent being told what to do. Most people resent being told how to live. But—as in so much else—Christians are to be different to most people. The Bible instructs us on how to live to please God. And it is there for us to obey...

More and more

⏵ **Read 1 Thessalonians 4 v 1-2**

Paul starts by acknowledging that the Thessalonians are living to please God. But then he asks and urges them to do this more and more. And, as an apostle, he does so with the authority of King Jesus Himself.

apply

Spend a few moments thinking about how your life is already orientated towards pleasing God. Give thanks to God for these encouragements.

Now, list at least three ways in which this needs to be the case "more and more".

Spend time praying through these different ways, asking for God's help today.

Living to please God

⏵ **Read v 3-8**

❓ What is God's will? (See v 3.)

❓ What is God's call? (See v 7.)

Christians can often get very concerned about the question of guidance. But, by putting things very simply, Paul gives us general principles to apply to every decision we make.

❓ Are there issues about which you have recently been seeking guidance?

❓ How does the simplicity of God's will and God's call help you?

Avoid sexual immorality

Then, as now, one of the key battlegrounds for the Christian is sexual morality.

❓ How are Christians to be different?

❓ Why are Christians to be different?

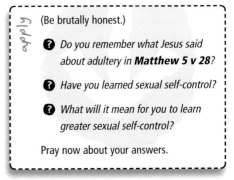

apply

(Be brutally honest.)

❓ Do you remember what Jesus said about adultery in **Matthew 5 v 28**?

❓ Have you learned sexual self-control?

❓ What will it mean for you to learn greater sexual self-control?

Pray now about your answers.

Now about brotherly love

O n the night before He died, Jesus spoke to His disciples: "A new command I give you: Love one another. As I have loved you, so you must love one another. By this all men will know that you are my disciples, if you love one another" (John 13 v 34-35).

▶ Read 1 Thessalonians 4 v 9-12

❓ How have the Thessalonians been getting on in this regard?

More and more

❓ What exactly is Paul urging in v 10?

❓ What three things does Paul commend in v 11?

❓ What will be the two results (v 12)?

❓ What is the link between v 11 and v 12?

apply

❓ How should the lives of Christians be seen to be different from the lives of non-Christians?

apply

❓ How is this truth worked out in your life at this time?

Spend time talking to God about your answers.

time out

We know that Christians are to love one another. Spend a few moments now flicking to the verses below, and reflecting on our responsibilities to one another.

Romans 12 v 10

Ephesians 4 v 32

Colossians 3 v 13

Colossians 3 v 16

Hebrews 10 v 24

Labours of love

Back in 1 v 3, we see Paul giving thanks for (among other things) the way the Thessalonians' love prompted them to labour. This reminds us that Christian love is no wishy-washy emotion, or here-today-gone-tomorrow feeling. Love prompts labour.

Hope that inspires

▶ Reading: 1 Thessalonians 4 v 13-18   **Wednesday** 12 October

P art of the authentic Christian life involves waiting—waiting for Jesus to return from heaven (1 v 10). But what happens if Christians die before Jesus returns?

▶ Read 1 Thessalonians 4 v 13-18

Hope in the face of grief

❓ *When fellow Christians die, why do we not grieve as those who have no hope?*

❓ *What is the problem with being ignorant about this?*

Of course, it is very different when a non-Christian dies. Paul's second letter to the Thessalonians reminds us that those who do not know God and who do not obey the gospel will be punished with everlasting destruction and shut out from Jesus' presence (**2 Thessalonians 1 v 8-9**).

But this should not blind us to the security of all those who "fall asleep" in Christ...

The coming of the Lord

❓ *At the coming of the Lord, in what order will events happen?*

❓ *Why does this give us cause for hope?*

Thinking back to 1 v 3, we saw how endurance is inspired by hope.

❓ *How does this hope inspire us to endure?*

"And so we will be with the Lord for ever." It's a short sentence, but with profound implications.

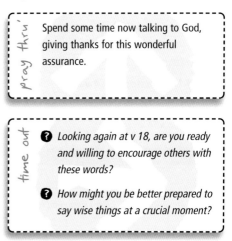

pray thru' Spend some time now talking to God, giving thanks for this wonderful assurance.

time out
❓ *Looking again at v 18, are you ready and willing to encourage others with these words?*

❓ *How might you be better prepared to say wise things at a crucial moment?*

BIBLE IN A YEAR: **SONG OF SONGS 6-8 • EPHESIANS 2**

Coming! Ready or not...

The Old Testament prophets had warned that the day of the Lord would be a divisive day. For those who rejected God, it would be a day of terrible wrath. For those who trusted God, it would be a day of wonderful vindication. And so it really matters whether or not we are ready for it...

The day of the Lord

▶ **Read 1 Thessalonians 5 v 1-3**

❷ What did the Thessalonians "know very well"?

❷ What point is Paul making by referring to a thief in the night?

❷ What point is Paul making by referring to a pregnant woman's labour pains?

And yet some will still be saying: "Peace and safety"! Here's a reminder of the danger of false teaching: it gives people false assurance, telling them they are safe when in fact they are in extreme danger.

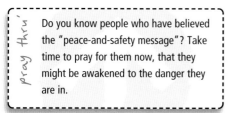

pray thru   Do you know people who have believed the "peace-and-safety message"? Take time to pray for them now, that they might be awakened to the danger they are in.

We belong to the day

▶ **Read v 4-11**

❷ Why will the day of the Lord not surprise us?

❷ How should we prepare for it?

❷ Why can Christians be confident that we will not face God's wrath?

time out   **Spend some time looking again at verse 8.**

❷ In what ways do you need to take note of this encouragement to be self-controlled?

❷ How do faith, hope and love act as your armour for the spiritual battle?

apply   Verse 11 is very specific: "Therefore encourage one another and build each other up, just as in fact you are doing."

❷ Who will you encourage and build up?

❷ How will you do this in the coming days?

Loving God's people

▶ **Reading:** 1 Thessalonians 5 v 12-15   **Friday** 14 October

*L*iving the life of faith, love and hope will not always be easy. We will need to help each other, and also put up with each other!

❓ *Think of your church for a moment.*

- *How would you describe it?*

- *What attitudes prevail?*

- *What issues are important?*

As Paul comes towards the end of his letter, he now gives specific instructions relating to our church life together...

▶ **Read 1 Thessalonians 5 v 12-15**

Respecting church leaders

Christian leaders are (among other things) to work hard, and to admonish us.

❓ *How can you show that you respect them as they do this?*

❓ *What will it mean for you to "hold them in the highest regard in love"?*

❓ *Why are church leaders often not respected as they should be?*

> *time out*
>
> **Hebrews 13 v 7** and **v 17** say more about how we should relate to our church leaders.
>
> ❓ *What different commands are given?*
>
> ❓ *How might you set an example of obedience in this area in your church?*

Supporting church members

❓ *What attitudes should dominate our church life?*

❓ *How would you distinguish between the idle, the timid, and the weak?*

❓ *To what extent is your church's life typified by kindness?*

❓ *Which of these commands do you find the greatest personal challenge?*

Take time now to pray about your answers.

> *pray thru'*
>
> ❓ *Are there things you need to confess here?*
>
> If so, take time to pray now.

And finally…

▶ **Reading:** 1 Thessalonians 5 v 16-28   **Saturday** 15 October

Faith, love and hope have been the key themes in 1 Thessalonians. Last time we thought about our **love** for God's people. Today we're going to look at our **faith** in God's provision and our **hope** in God's promises.

Faith in God's provision

▶ **Read 1 Thessalonians 5 v 16-22**

❓ Why are joyfulness, prayerfulness, and thankfulness (v 16-18) all good indicators of our faith in God's provision?

❓ Which of the three do you find the greatest challenge?

❓ Why do you think this is?

Of course, the greatest way in which God provides for us is by enabling us to know Him personally. By His Spirit, through His word, we come to know God's character and purposes. And so, as the Bible is the sword of the Spirit, we must be careful not to put out the Spirit's fire (v 19). And we must take great care as we listen to those who would seek to teach us (v 20-22).

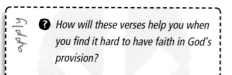

apply

❓ How will these verses help you when you find it hard to have faith in God's provision?

Hope in God's promises

▶ **Read v 23-28**

❓ What will God do?

❓ How can we know He will do it?

❓ Given all that God has promised to do, how should we respond to Him?

Take time to talk to Him now.

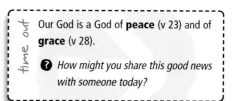

time out

Our God is a God of **peace** (v 23) and of **grace** (v 28).

❓ How might you share this good news with someone today?

Anxiety attack 1

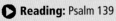

▶ **Reading:** Psalm 139   **Sunday** 16 October

This great song needs no introduction, except to say it's wonderful!

▶ **Read Psalm 139**

Do you agree?

Verses 19-22 are the clue to what's going on here. David is under attack by people who hate God and hate him. Scared, he stops to remember just how secure he is in God's hands.

God knows me

▶ **Read v 1-6**

❓ *How well does God know David (and therefore each of us)?*

❓ *What specifically does David recognise that God knows (v 4-6)?*

Such knowledge (v 5) might be terrifying, leading to paranoia, but v 6 shows that David doesn't feel trapped by his lack of privacy from God.

God is everywhere

▶ **Read v 7-10**

David isn't trying to escape from God. Rather, he's just saying: "It's impossible to escape from God—even if I wanted to". High up (v 8a), low down (v 8b), east (v 9a), west (v 9b)...

See what David realised?

---

time out

There are times when we just want to run away... Sometimes, it's because we're harbouring some secret sin that we don't want to be exposed to the Lord's disapproving (but loving) stare. Sometimes, we're just afraid of intimacy. But at other times, it all just gets too much for us. Pressures and demands, being squeezed into a life that you didn't choose by work, family, friends and church. We lose our nerve, and toy with the idea of running away from it all...

It may be good, if you can, to have a holiday from all the pressures, but it's just plain silly to think we can run away from God. And often, when we're under pressure, we lose the vital perspective that the God who knows us, also loves us with a deep, caring and gentle passion.

Read John 6 v 66-69.

God is in control

▶ **Read v 4**

This verse raises a problem for many people... If God knows everything about me, aren't I just a robot with no free will? **1 Peter 2 v 9-12** gives us a clue. God chooses His people in His mercy, so that they will praise Him. And that's a response that can only come from the heart. God is in control, yet He wants us to freely give Him honour.

❓ *Will you complain about His power, or praise Him for His mercy? Do one or the other now...*

Daniel: Staying faithful

Welcome to the book of Daniel. After covering the first half in the last issue of Explore, we're diving back in halfway through.

So it's well worth reminding ourselves of the main themes of the book...

The book of Daniel is set in Babylon, where Daniel and his friends have been taken into exile.

▶ **Read Daniel 3 v 8-12, 6 v 10-14**

❓ *What challenges have Daniel and his friends faced?*

▶ **Read 3 v 28-29, 6 v 26-27**

❓ *What have been some of the main lessons in living for God so far?*

▶ **Read 2 v 46-47, 5 v 22-28**

❓ *What have been some of the main lessons about God Himself so far?*

The book of Daniel is all about living faithfully for God in a pagan land. It is at a time when God's people are in exile and so God appears to have been defeated. But the main theme is: *God remains the true God, so stay faithful to Him.*

So the first six chapters see Daniel and his friends living faithfully for God, even when under pressure not to, and being rescued and vindicated for doing so. And we've seen pagan kings being brought to recognise God as the true God.

time out

It's sometimes hard to see how Daniel's experience of the world can have much to do with ours. Most of us aren't Jewish, pining for a return to Israel. None of us are serving a Babylonian king while trying to live for God.

But in the New Testament, Peter describes Christians as *"strangers in the world, scattered"* throughout the earth (1 Peter 1 v 1). None of us are yet living in the ultimate land of heaven. All of us face the daily tension of living for God in a world which doesn't recognise or respect Him.

In fact, Daniel's world isn't so very different from our own!

apply

❓ *In your own life, where are the tensions between how everyone expects you to act, and how God tells you to act?*

Peter says Christians have *"an inheritance that can never perish, spoil or fade—kept in heaven for you"* (1 Peter 1 v 4).

❓ *Is that what you're most looking forward to today?*

pray thru'

Pray that as you spend the next few weeks in Daniel, the true God would be encouraging, equipping and challenging you to stay faithful to Him.

A look ahead

18

T*he stories of the first six chapters of Daniel are often taught in Sunday school and in sermons. The second half of the book is usually left alone! We're going to work our way through it, but it's worth taking a moment to understand more about how to read this section of the Bible.*

So today's study isn't really a study—it's a (hopefully!) helpful introduction.

A clear structure

▶ **Read Daniel 7 v 1**

❓ *What's curious about the timing here (look back to 5 v 30-31)?*

In terms of time, chapter 7 is placed between chapters 4 and 5. In other words, having finished the events of chapters 1–6 we now rewind to read about Daniel's dreams. Chapters 1 – 6 and 7 – 12 have been structured to form two overlapping sections.

Similar but different

▶ **Read verses 15-18**

❓ *What's happening to Daniel here?*

These are much like what was going on in chapter 2 (it might be worth taking a couple of minutes to read through it)—but now Daniel is the one who has the dreams. And he has to be told what they mean, rather than interpreting them himself.

There is also more about the political powers of the ancient world and how they relate to God. But the difference is

that God doesn't intervene as obviously and directly as he does in the first six chapters. His people often suffer for faithfulness rather than being saved miraculously. Arrogant kings seem to prosper rather than being humbled.

The same theme

The theme of the book is still the same, however: God remains the true God so stay faithful to Him. And faithfulness often means suffering persecution, even death, while waiting for God's promises to be fulfilled.

Apocalyptic now

The content of the dreams is in symbolic language (technically it's called "apocalyptic" writing), where the objects stand for certain things. Some of these are clearly interpreted for us—for example, look at 8 v 20.

We're not familiar with this kind of writing today. We need to remember that despite being a bit weird, it is simply a symbolic audio-visual display to Daniel; there's nothing particularly mysterious about it. That's not to say it's all easy to understand, mind you— but the general idea is straightforward enough.

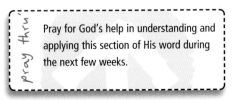

pray thru" Pray for God's help in understanding and applying this section of His word during the next few weeks.

Kings and beasts

▶ **Reading:** Daniel 7 v 1-7, 15-17   **Wednesday** 19 October

The world of Daniel's dreams revolves around God and human rulers/kingdoms. But these are described using the animal world.

The interpreter dreams

▶ **Read Daniel 7 v 1, 15-16**

Daniel, who has interpreted everyone else's dreams, now has some dreams of his own; he knows they are significant, and so he writes them down. This dream is different in that it comes supplied with its own interpreter!

So, the chapter divides into two: the first half is the description of what Daniel sees and hears; the second half is the interpretation of what it all means (with some extra detail given about the vision).

The four beasts

▶ **Read Daniel 7 v 2-7, 17**

❓ What are these beasts?

❓ Where do they come from?

❓ Try to picture each beast in turn—what ideas and feelings do they bring to your mind?

Verse 17 tells us that these beasts represent different kingdoms that will come in the future. They all come out of the sea, which in the Bible is seen as a place of chaos and evil—this is why there'll be no more sea in the new creation (Revelation 21 v 1). So these are earthly kingdoms which are evil in character.

Each kingdom has its own particular features: for example, the first is fierce like a lion and swift like an eagle. It becomes a more "human" empire, meaning it is less savage and evil.

God's sovereignty

Despite the frightening appearance of these animal-like creatures, we still see God's authority over them. The first has its wings torn off but is "given" the heart of a man. The second is "told" to eat. The third is "given" authority to rule. Within the chaos and evil, God is still in control.

---

apply

❓ How does this passage shape our thinking about evil empires and rulers that we see around us today?

❓ Why do you think God revealed this to Daniel?

The fourth kingdom

*W*e've seen the start of Daniel's vision of different beasts which represent different kingdoms. However, the real focus of the chapter is on the fourth kingdom.

A horrible sight

▶ **Read Daniel 7 v 7, 19-23**

❓ *What is different about this fourth kingdom?*

❓ *How do you think we are we supposed to feel as we read this?*

The fourth kingdom is clearly different—Daniel can't compare it with any identifiable animal. It is frightening, vicious and devastating. The interpretation tells us it will dominate the world.

Part of the purpose of this symbolic language is that it makes us feel things as well as know things. We should, with Daniel, feel awed and horrified at this vision.

A horrible ruler

▶ **Read verses 8, 24-25**

The horns represent particular rulers, so here a new ruler comes up within the ten that were present previously.

❓ *What are we told this ruler is like (v 24)?*

❓ *What will he do (v 21, 25)?*

This little horn speaks boastfully—which in Daniel is a bad move to make (**see Daniel 4 v 28-33**)! The interpretation tells us this will means speaking against

God and fighting His people. Changing the "set times and the laws" (v 25) means stopping the sacrificial system and holy days in Israel.

This refers to a Greek ruler called Antiochus Epiphanes, who lived in the second century BC. Just as the vision suggests, he emerged from ten kings of the Greek empire. He specifically persecuted Jews in Israel in just this way. The next chapters will focus on him and his tyranny specifically.

apply

We've seen that governments are given authority by God and can exercise His rule in the world. Here we see a government and ruler becoming horribly evil and being little more than a tool for Satan.

❓ *Why do you think God reveals this to His people ahead of time?*

❓ *What mistakes in thinking does it help us avoid?*

❓ *Why is it encouraging to know that God is in charge even when appearances suggest He isn't?*

God comes on the scene

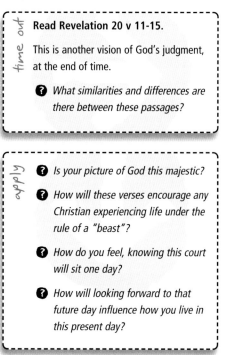

W*e've seen the four animals picturing four different kingdoms, with the focus on the fourth kingdom and on a particular ruler. But partway through, the vision changes.*

The heavenly court

Read Daniel 7 v 9-10

? *What sort of scene is being described here?*

? *What details are we given?*

? *What should we feel as we read this description?*

This is like a heavenly courtroom in which God comes and sits as judge. He is the "Ancient of Days", showing He's not limited by time. The colour of His clothes and hair symbolise purity. The details about His throne symbolise His judgment. Millions of people are gathered around Him.

The beasts were scary in their ferocity—but this is scary in a different way. This is God enthroned in majestic splendour, far more powerful than the beasts.

? *What's the last thing to be described in verse 10?*

The court is now ready and "the books were opened". This is God sitting in judgment—and the books are the records or accounts of people's lives and actions.

The bringing of judgment

Read verses 11-12, 26

? *What happens to the beast with the "little horn"?*

This is a picture of judgment and punishment on that ruler and kingdom. We must be careful in saying when this happens, because in verse 12 the previous kingdoms are still in existence. There is a flow of history here and there is a stepping out of time (but that sort thing can happen in dreams!).

---

time out

Read Revelation 20 v 11-15.

This is another vision of God's judgment, at the end of time.

? *What similarities and differences are there between these passages?*

---

apply

? *Is your picture of God this majestic?*

? *How will these verses encourage any Christian experiencing life under the rule of a "beast"?*

? *How do you feel, knowing this court will sit one day?*

? *How will looking forward to that future day influence how you live in this present day?*

The true ruler

*D*aniel's vision so far has involved different kingdoms, one specific ruler and God's heavenly court of judgment. But there's one last figure who's part of the action, and who we haven't yet looked at...

The "son of man"

Read Daniel 7 v 13-14

? *What happens to this person?*

? *What is said about him?*

The figure is "like" a son of man—just as the previous figures were "like" a lion and so on. "Son of man" is a way of saying "a human". So Daniel simply sees someone like a human being appear.

But *this* human is riding on the clouds—which is what God does (see Psalm 104 v 3). This human is led into the presence of God as if he belongs there. And he is given "authority, glory and sovereign power". This is like a coronation ceremony or enthronement of a king. And this king will be worshipped by absolutely everyone, and his kingdom will last forever. These are phrases that the Bible only uses of God.

God's Ruler

In the Old Testament, God's rule was through His king. His king was granted authority and power and ruled for God. So this figure in Daniel 7 is God's ultimate King.

This is the man we know as Jesus, God's anointed King. This is Jesus being enthroned and worshipped as He rules a kingdom that will never end. We'll look more at how the New Testament links this passage to Jesus in the next study.

time out

People often talk of Jesus as their "best friend". And there's nothing wrong with Christians seeing Jesus in this way: but that should never be the *only* way we think of Him.

? *How does this passage enlarge our view of Jesus beyond "best friend"?*

pray thru'

See the conqueror mounts in triumph,
See the King in royal state
Riding on the clouds his chariot
To his heavenly palace gate;
Hark the choirs of angel voices
Joyful hallelujahs sing,
And the portals high are lifted
To receive their heavenly King.

Who is this that comes in glory,
With the trump of jubilee?
Lord of battles, God of armies,
He had gained the victory;
He who on the cross did suffer,
He who from the grave arose,
He has vanquished sin and Satan,
He by death has spoiled his foes.

Christopher Wordsworth

Choose some of these phrases to help you praise Jesus, the Son of Man, now.

Anxiety attack 2

▶ **Reading:** Psalm 139 (again) **Sunday** 23 October

I t's such a great psalm, we'll have two bites at the cherry.

▶ **Read Psalm 139**

Do you still agree it's brilliant?

God is in control

▶ **Read v 13-18**

❓ *How is it that God knows David so well (v 13)?*

❓ *Why is David praising God in v 14-15?*

All the more remarkable when you think that David never saw a scan of a baby in the womb.

❓ *So what's so surprising about v 16b?*

---

time out

The media is full of public discussion about issues of medical ethics.

❓ *What do verses 13-18 have to say about the value of human life?*

❓ *What would you say on the basis of these verses to a pregnant woman who suspects that the child she is carrying is disabled in some way?*

---

pray thru'

It's easier to advise than to be in the situation. Spend some time praying for mothers, families, and Christian medical staff who face these difficult situations. Pray that they would know the truth of these verses and believe in the God who knows and cares.

Commitment

▶ **Read v 19-24**

Has David flipped here? From profound and intimate thoughts about God, he's suddenly gone all aggressive. Well, David is honest if nothing else. He's desperate for people to honour God, and he doesn't shrink from saying what he feels in prayer to God.

❓ *He recognises that God knows him, is everywhere and is in total control, so how does David pray (v 23-24)?*

❓ *What's the link with verses 1 and 2?*

---

apply

God knows all there is to know about you (even stuff you don't know). But He still has a firm hold on us to lead and protect us...

So we can live as His enemy, trying to escape him (stupidity).

Or we can trust Him in His knowledge and power (security).

Read the psalm through again as a prayer, as though you'd written it yourself...

The Son of Man

We've looked at the appearance of this awesome figure who is "like a son of man": our Lord Jesus. In this study we'll take a moment to see some of Jesus' comments about Himself as this figure of Daniel 7.

Read Daniel 7 v 13-14

Now look up the following references, and for each one think about how Jesus is referring to Daniel 7 to help us see more of who He is:

- **Matthew 16 v 27-28**

- **Matthew 24 v 30-31**

- **Matthew 26 v 64**

A two-stage enthronement

Jesus says that some people will see Him exalted and enthroned in their own lifetime; and that happened in His resurrection and ascension. In that way He was exalted and His kingdom came.

But not everyone saw that, and not all the world worshipped Him. His kingdom hadn't *fully* come. But one day He will return, everyone will bow before Him, and His kingdom will never end.

We live between Jesus' exaltation and the enforcement of His rule. We live in the time when people can come under the rule of God's King willingly; we live after He died to offer a way into His kingdom, and before He returns to judge His enemies.

Telling of God's King

Read Matthew 28 v 18-20

? How does verse 18 echo Daniel 7?

? What command does this exalted King give His people (v 19-20)?

? How does the truth of verse 18 means it's right that Christians get on with doing verses 19-20?

Jesus has been given all authority. And so now everyone on earth should become a disciple of King Jesus, for their sake but also for His, so that He is given the respect His position deserves and demands.

Pray thru

Spend a few moments bowing before Jesus and praising God that He has exalted His King.

Pray for your own efforts in telling others of God's King. Name some friends or family members who don't know Jesus as their Lord, and ask God for opportunities, courage and the right words to talk to them about Him.

And we shall reign with Him

▶ **Reading:** Daniel 7 v 17-18, 21-22, 26-27   **Tuesday** 25 October

What an amazing chapter Daniel 7 is! We've seen the evil kingdoms of the world, and one ruler in particular, persecuting God's people. We've seen God's heavenly court and the arrival of the Son of Man, who will rule. But there's one last aspect we haven't looked at yet—the incredible truth that we will rule with Him!

The turnaround

▶ **Read Daniel 7 v 17-18**

❓ *What summary of the whole dream do these verses give?*

▶ **Read verses 21-22**

❓ *What dramatic change takes place in these verses?*

The giving of the kingdom

▶ **Read verses 26-27**

❓ *What is given to God's people here?*

❓ *How does this make you feel?*

We see again that the world will be dominated by earthly kingdoms, and that will involve God's people suffering persecution. That's not a surprise to us as we look around this world. What's simply amazing is that the wonderful day will come when:

• God's court will sit, judge those evil powers and remove their authority

• God will vindicate His people

• God will give His people the kingdom

Back where we're meant to be

Mankind was created to be God's rulers on earth. **Psalm 8** tells us that people were "crowned with glory and honour" (v 5). The way humans rule is now distorted and often evil, but God plans to restore us to that place. He does so through Jesus, the perfect man. Jesus is the one who will rule and reign for God (Daniel 7 v 14)—and if we are His people, He shares His rule with us (v 27).

---

time out

The apocalyptic New Testament book of Revelation shares many themes with this part of Daniel.

Read Revelation 22 v 1-5.

❓ *What links this vision of the future with Daniel's?*

❓ *Do you spot any other Old Testament references in these verses?*

---

pray thru'

The hymn we looked at last Saturday about Jesus' exaltation continues:

He has raised our human nature
In the clouds to God's right hand;
There we sit in heavenly places,
There with him in glory stand;
Jesus reigns, adored by angels;
Man with God is on the throne;
Mighty Lord, in your ascension,
We by faith behold our own.

Again, use a couple of these lines to prompt your praise of the Son of Man.

Hard times ahead

▶ **Reading:** Daniel 8 v 1-12, 15-27

Having worked through Daniel 7, *chapter 8 shouldn't be so daunting (although it has its tricky bits!). It helps to bear in mind that "animals" represent kings or kingdoms, and "horns" represent specific kings.*

Political movements

▶ **Read Daniel 8 v 1-8, 15-22**

Here is a more specific account of some of the kingdoms we saw in the last chapter. The kingdom of Media and Persia is represented by the two-horned ram—the Persian side was stronger, represented by the longer horn.

But this kingdom was defeated by the rise of the Greek kingdom. The large horn—the first king of Greece—is Alexander the Great. His military domination was extraordinarily swift (v 5); but at the height of his power he died and his kingdom was divided between four of his generals (v 8).

Back to the "little horn"

▶ **Read verses 9-12, v 23-27**

❓ *What is described here that we also saw in chapter 7?*

❓ *What's the most shocking thing about this king (v 11)?*

❓ *Why do you think Daniel reacts as he does to what he's seen and heard (v 27)?*

From one of the four kingdoms comes a specific ruler who attacks the "beautiful land"—that is, Israel. This is Antiochus

Epiphanes, who we came across earlier—he persecuted Jews, stopped sacrifices being offered and desecrated the temple.

His actions are presented in terms of attacking the "starry host". This is a way of speaking about God's people, but it shows there is more than an earthly struggle going on—this is a fight in the heavenly realms (more on that later in the book).

This king sets himself up to be as great as the "Prince of the host" (v 11)—which is God Himself. This king takes his stand against the "Prince of princes" (v 25). This is an earthly king making himself god.

❓ *Will his bid to rival and topple God succeed (v 25)?*

> *pray thru'* Pray for Christian brothers and sisters around the world who are suffering persecution at the hands of human rulers today. Pray that they would not be "thrown down" by losing their faith.
>
> Information can be found online at **www.persecution.org**

How long O Lord?

▶ **Reading:** Daniel 8 v 13-14   **Thursday** 27 October

W e've seen the big sweep of Daniel's vision of chapter 8; now we're looking at the details of timing.

Political movements

▶ **Read Daniel 8 v 13-14**

❓ *What question is being asked and answered here?*

❓ *Why would this question have mattered so much to Daniel?*

Daniel wants to know how long the devastation of the temple in Jerusalem will last—with the associated horrors of the sacrifices being ended and the trampling of God's people underfoot. How long will this persecution be?

The answer comes in verse 14. We know from other sources roughly how long the desecration of the temple was—the exact figure is debated, but it was approximately this time period.

Symbolism?

Back in chapter 7 we were told how long God's people would be handed over to this evil king. It was "a time, times and half a time" (7 v 25). That's a way of adding up to three and half. It could mean three-and-a-half years, but this becomes a symbolic number representing a time of persecution. We see the same number used in the book of Revelation about the persecution of the church (**Revelation 12 v 6, 14**).

The number in Daniel 8 is a bit shorter than three and half years. Maybe it is the precise timing, maybe it's an approximation. But the point being made here is that...

God is still in control

God's people, in Daniel's day and in ours, ask God: "How long?" for two reasons. The first reason is because what they are talking about is terrible and they want to know when it will end. But the second reason is because they believe God is in control and can bring it to an end. There's no point asking that question of someone who doesn't know and can't do anything about it.

Saying: "How long?" is a cry of anguish—but it's also a cry of faith.

apply

❓ *In what ways would the details here have reassured Daniel, and those who read these words at the time?*

❓ *In what ways does it reassure you?*

❓ *When you are facing difficult circumstances, do you turn to God and speak openly with Him about how you're feeling?*

If there's something you're worried about or scared of that you've been keeping from God, wouldn't this be a good time to talk to Him about it?

Sovereignty and prayer

Reading: Daniel 9 v 1-3

28

There's a brief break from Daniel's visions for us to hear him pray (although at the end of his prayer comes another vision!) But before we look at his prayer, it's worth thinking about why Daniel is praying at all.

Discovery

⏵ **Read Daniel 9 v 1-3**

❓ *When is this set?*

❓ *What does Daniel find out, and where from?*

❓ *How does this encourage or challenge you?*

---

time out

It's lovely to see this giant of the faith, who has his own Bible book, humbly sitting down with God's word and seeking to understand and apply it to his life: just as Christians do today, and just as you are doing right now!

What a great encouragement to be people who search the Scriptures day by day, as we seek to follow God as Daniel did!

⏵ **Read Jeremiah 25 v 8-14**

❓ *What is described here?*

❓ *What is the key point that Daniel discovers?*

God speaks through Jeremiah, explaining why the exile would come and what it would involve... and how long it would last—70 years.

Prayer

⏵ **Read Daniel 9 v 4**

❓ *Why do you think this discovery results in prayer?*

❓ *How does Daniel pray?*

This is no throwaway, one-sentence prayer. Daniel is pleading with God; and he is showing the attitude of his heart with outward signs like not eating and wearing sackcloth. This is not a prayer of celebration; it's a prayer of confession.

---

apply

❓ *How often are your prayers based on what you have read in the Bible and applied to your life?*

❓ *Do your prayers regularly include confessing how you've sinned?*

It's amazing that Daniel prays at all! He hears that the exile will last 70 years—so he could sit back and wait. Instead he falls on his knees and (as we'll see) prays the exile will end as God has promised.

How God's sovereignty and our prayers fit together is never explained to us—but we're told to pray for what God has promised. So there's no doubt God's kingdom will come—each day as God works, and finally, when His Son returns —but still Jesus tells us to pray for it.

---

apply

❓ *What have you learned about how to pray from Daniel's example here?*

Take some minutes to talk to God now...

BIBLE IN A YEAR: **2 SAMUEL 9-11** • **1 JOHN 2**

Telling it like it is

▶ **Reading:** Daniel 9 v 4-14   **Saturday** 29 October

W*e overhear Daniel in prayer here. He's praying about the sin of his people and it's not pretty, but it is real. Daniel is telling it like it is.*

What they've done

▶ **Read Daniel 9 v 4-14**

Look for all the things that Daniel says he and his people have done.

❓ *How does he describe himself and his people?*

What God's done

Look for all the things that Daniel says God has done.

❓ *How does he describe God?*

The history of Israel is being described here. It's a history of constant turning away from God; regular disobedience of God; and repeated ignoring of God's warnings. So Daniel uses words like "wicked", "unfaithful" and "shame".

God, however, is described as "awesome", "righteous" and "merciful". God has done nothing wrong—He has borne with His people and He has repeatedly warned them. But eventually He has punished them—and He was right to do so.

apply

❓ *How does this prayer guide us in how to confess to God as His people today?*

❓ *Compare Daniel's prayer of confession to yours. Any changes you need to make?*

time out

What's striking about Daniel's prayer is not only its searing honesty, but also its "corporate" nature.

Read Nehemiah 1 v 5-7.

Both Daniel and Nehemiah (a little later in history) remember that they are part of the people of God; and they accept that they are responsible in some part for that people's sin. They avoid the mistake of relating to God only as an individual, rather than seeing their life as tied up with the life of God's people. And they avoid the error of bemoaning the weaknesses of the rest of God's people (in our day, the Christian church), while forgetting that their own personal sin contributes to those weaknesses.

❓ *How do these examples help you to confess your sins individually, but as part of God's people?*

pray thru'

Since we've been looking at a prayer of confession, take a few moments to confess now to God your sin, and the sins of God's people.

Use Daniel's prayer to shape yours (it might prove helpful to write yours down first).

Double trouble

30

▶ **Reading:** Psalm 140   **Sunday** 30 October

Trouble comes in a number of forms. There's the one-time crisis—a bolt of lightning from a clear blue sky—knocking us down when we least expect it. And there is the steady, relentless grind of insoluble difficulties that dog our steps for years.

❓ *Do you cope differently with these stresses? Which would you prefer to have?*

Hard times can easily detach us from God and godly living. Psalms 140 – 143 will show us how David coped with wave after wave of agony.

▶ **Read Psalm 140**

Slandered...

❓ *What is David's first reaction to trouble?*

It's a mark of the genuine believer. Some people pick up the phone and complain to their friends—some just run away. Others turn to the bottle or pills. The Christian instinct is to turn first to God.

> **time out**
>
> Tea and sympathy with Christian friends can have great restorative value (beware of the gossip factor, however). And sometimes it's right to seek medical advice for help (we don't recommend boozing your way out of trouble, however). But David's instinct is surely right: turn to God and pray.
>
> ❓ *Is this your reaction when trouble lands on your doorstep?*

...but safe

▶ **Read v 6-13**

❓ *What does David pray for himself (v 1-5)?*

❓ *And what does he pray for those who slander him (v 8-11)?*

❓ *List the truths about God he hangs on to in v 6-7 and 12-13. We count at least seven— maybe you can find more...*

God is...

❓ *And how does this knowledge of God's character, ability and past deeds help David (see v 12-13)?*

> **pray thru'**
>
> Turn your list into praise and prayer, asking God (who is *your* God) to help you remember correctly, and respond rightly in times of crisis.

Pleading with God

▶ **Reading:** Daniel 9 v 15-19   **Monday** 31 October

Having confessed the sin of his people, Daniel turns to asking God to do something. And once again, he sets a pattern for us.

Content of prayer

▶ **Read Daniel 9 v 15-17**

❓ What does Daniel ask God to do?

❓ What does Daniel continue to admit about himself and the rest of God's people?

Daniel is praying for the restoration of Jerusalem. That is, the re-establishment of God's kingdom: His rule, in His land, over His people. That restoration will mean God forgiving, turning from His wrath and acting to restore.

time out

Jerusalem was the centre of God's kingdom because it contained His temple, where He dwelled, the place where He could be met with and where forgiveness could be found; the place God's people longed to be established and glorified.

But supremely, God dwelled on earth not in a place but in a person. Since we live after God's Son came into this world, we meet and find forgiveness from God in Him. The Lord Jesus is the ruler and centre of God's kingdom.

❓ What does this mean about what "the establishment of God's kingdom" looks like today?

❓ How should this shape our prayers?

Reasons for prayer

▶ **Read verses 17-19**

❓ What reasons does Daniel give as to why he thinks God should answer his prayer?

Daniel is clear here—their sin means they have don't deserve God's restoration in any way. So he makes these requests because of God's mercy, and for the sake of God's name, His reputation.

apply

❓ What "reasons" do you tend to offer to God as to why He should answer your prayers?

It needs to be His mercy and His glory that are the basis for your requests: not anything you have done.

pray thru'

Again, let Daniel's prayers form the pattern for yours. As you pray now, follow Daniel in *what* you pray for, the *basis* on which you ask for those things, and the *manner* in which you pray.

Longer time, greater result

D aniel's prayer gets interrupted rather unusually by an answer from God—and we're back to the vision language of chapters 7 and 8.

An answer given

▶ Read Daniel 9 v 20-23

❓ How does verse 20 sum up the first part of the chapter?

❓ What are all Daniel's requests focused on (end of verse 20)?

❓ Why does Gabriel say he has come?

A revised timing

▶ Read verse 24

❓ How long does Gabriel say the exile will take?

❓ Daniel reads in Jeremiah 25 8-14 of "seventy years" of exile. How do you think he felt about the new timing outlined in this verse?

Daniel is being told that it is not as simple as the exile being over in seventy years. We must remember that the exile wasn't only being out of the land—it was a statement about people's relationship with God, not just where they lived. So it was possible to be back in the land of Israel, but to still be in "exile".

In **Leviticus 26 v 14-35**, God warns His people that if they disobey and ignore Him, they won't live in the land—they will be punished "seven times over" while the land enjoys "Sabbath rest" ie: the life with God that people could enjoy if they did not sin. It may well be that "seven", both here and in Daniel 9, is a symbolic number meaning "complete".

An greater result

▶ Re-read verse 24

❓ What will happen at the end of this time?

Daniel was expecting a return to Jerusalem and rebuilding of the temple. But God promises much more than that! The first three of this list are to do with the end of sin in its penalty and presence: the end of what caused the exile.

The second three look beyond that: the arrival of righteousness (a right relationship with God and a right way of living), the "sealing" or fulfilment of God's promises, and the anointing of a holy place. The "holy place" was the temple in Jerusalem—God dwelling with his people.

But the temple didn't deliver what's pictured here—the end of sin and the fulfilment of all of God's plans. These are things that are only fulfilled in the ultimate "holy place", the person of Jesus. And Daniel is being told that while the physical exile will end after 70 years, the end to spiritual exile will take a lot longer. But, amazingly, it will happen!

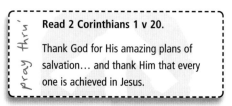

pray thru'

Read 2 Corinthians 1 v 20.

Thank God for His amazing plans of salvation... and thank Him that every one is achieved in Jesus.

The abomination

Reading: Daniel 9 v 25-27   **Wednesday** 2 November

We've seen the start of God's answer to Daniel's prayer—that it will take longer for the exile to be truly over but in time God's plans will be fulfilled. Now comes a more specific description of future events—and this is where it gets complicated (and debated!).

Dividing up the "sevens"

▶ Read Daniel 9 v 25-27

The period of 70 "sevens" is now divided into different sections.

1. 7 sevens from the "decree to restore and rebuild Jerusalem" to this rebuilding work being completed.

2. 62 sevens which end with the arrival of the "Anointed One" at the end of which he is "cut off and will have nothing".

3. 1 seven in which a ruler comes who destroys the city and the sanctuary. This is the guy who sets up the famous "abomination that causes desolation".

This has been the stuff of great debate! My understanding is that the time periods are not precise but symbolic and relate to:

1. The time from the decree given by Cyrus that Jews could go back and rebuild the temple (**Ezra 1 v 1-4**) to the building work being completed.

2. The time until Jesus coming, who is the "Anointed One" and who was cut off and had nothing (**see Isaiah 53 v 8**).

3. The time after Jesus when the Roman ruler Titus levelled Jerusalem and destroyed the temple. (Jesus seems to refer to this in quoting 9 v 27 in **Mark 13 v 14**.)

Seeing the point

❓ *Given that Daniel was expecting the exile to be over in 70 years, what do you think the point of this detail is?*

Daniel and his people needed to know that the return to the land wasn't the end of the story. Rather, even once back in the land, there would be further trouble for God's people. In fact there would even be a further desolation of the temple. But God's anointed one *would* come and God's plans *would* be fulfilled.

time out

❓ *How should we respond, knowing that hard times may lie ahead, but that God remains in control and His plans will be fulfilled?*

Turn your answers into both prayer and praise.

Beasts then and now

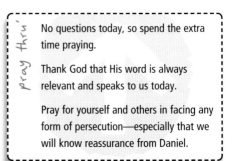

34

We take a moment out of working through Daniel to consider some of what we've been seeing.

Consider

- There has been repeated reference to kingdoms which will persecute God's people. These have often been represented as beasts (**7 v 21; 8 v 12; 8 v 24**).

- There has been repeated reference to "abominations" to do with the temple (**8 v 13; 9 v 27**).

- There has been repeated reference to a ruler who will exalt himself against God (**7 v 25; 8 v 11; 8 v 25**).

Real people

These references have real historical fulfilment in people like the Greek ruler Antiochus Epiphanes. He did persecute God's people, he did stop them offering sacrifices, and he did desecrate the temple (he set up an altar to Zeus in the temple and sacrificed a pig on it!). There was a later fulfilment when the Roman ruler Titus attacked Jerusalem and destroyed the temple.

Pictures of ongoing realities

However, presenting these events in symbolic language lifts them out of only one historical moment and makes them a pattern. This is one effect of this "apocalyptic" language.

So when the New Testament speaks about opposition to God's people and persecution, it uses the same imagery.

For example, in Revelation the beast that persecutes God's people in chapter 13 is a composite of pictures in Daniel. We read: *"He opened his mouth to blaspheme God, and to slander his name and his dwelling-place and those who live in heaven. He was given power to make war against the saints and to conquer them."* (**Revelation 13 v 6-7**)

This is describing the persecution under the Roman empire in the first century. But again it is lifted out of one historical setting and is set as the forces of evil against God and His people.

Reapplying today

So in reading Daniel (and Revelation), we can think of ways in which Satan persecutes Christians—often through particular rulers. We can reapply the same ideas we see in Daniel's day, and hear the same reassurances from God.

---

pray thru

No questions today, so spend the extra time praying.

Thank God that His word is always relevant and speaks to us today.

Pray for yourself and others in facing any form of persecution—especially that we will know reassurance from Daniel.

The vision

D*aniel's visions of the future aren't over and it's time for the last and longest of them. But this one (which will take us to the end of the book) has the longest introduction as well. Today we begin by seeing who is speaking to Daniel.*

A troubling revelation

▶ **Read Daniel 10 v 1-3**

❓ *What is Daniel's revelation about?*

❓ *How does Daniel respond to it?*

The revelation is about a war to come. We're told that the understanding of the revelation was made clear to Daniel through a vision, but there's a delay between the revelation and the vision. That's the time of v 2-3 where Daniel mourns for three weeks—presumably knowing enough to know what a terrible time it will be.

A startling vision

▶ **Read v 4-6**

❓ *Think through each element in the description and picture it.*

❓ *What is the overall impression given?*

An overwhelming reaction

▶ **Read v 7-9**

❓ *What effect does this vision have on Daniel's companions?*

❓ *What effect does this vision have on Daniel himself?*

Here is a vision of the Lord Jesus (we shouldn't really call him Jesus because that name was only given at His birth, but it's simpler to do so!). It is very similar to the description we get in **Revelation 1 v 13-16**, which you might like to read. Daniel, like John in Revelation, can't do anything but fall at His feet.

We are used to seeing Jesus as He appears in the Gospels—where He is an ordinary person. But we must remember that that was effectively Jesus in disguise. *This* is the real Jesus—awesome, glorious and mighty.

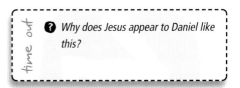

time out ❓ *Why does Jesus appear to Daniel like this?*

Daniel has seen a vision of a great war, a time of suffering when the world looks out of control and God seems to be absent. And what he needs more than explanation is the knowledge that God rules. This vision doesn't immediately give answers but it does give reassurance that God is mighty and powerful.

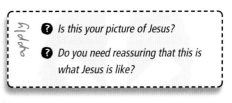

apply ❓ *Is this your picture of Jesus?*

❓ *Do you need reassuring that this is what Jesus is like?*

The spiritual battle

D*aniel's had a revelation and Jesus has arrived to interpret it to him. But before we get to the interpretation, Jesus explains why Daniel has been waiting so long. And, as a result, we get a fascinating insight into the spiritual battle around us.*

Heavenly hold-ups

▶ **Read Daniel 10 v 10-14**

❓ *What reassurance does Jesus give Daniel?*

❓ *Why was Jesus delayed?*

Jesus' touch and words set Daniel back on his feet. He is assured that Jesus has come to explain the vision he saw, and that the wait that he has had to endure means nothing negative about Daniel. In fact, Daniel's humble prayer for understanding was heard the day he started praying.

Jesus' delay was because of the "prince of the Persian kingdom". This is a reference to some spiritual being that relates to the kingdom of Persia (later we read about the prince of Greece).

The question

Given God's sovereignty we may wonder why Jesus should be delayed at all by any spiritual power.

▶ **Read Mark 1 v 23-27; 9 v 25-27; Colossians 2 v 9-10, 15**

❓ *What do these verses tell us about Jesus' authority?*

The New Testament makes it clear that Jesus has power and authority over evil spirits and all spiritual beings. So Daniel 10 v 13 **cannot** mean that this prince/king of Persia is more powerful than Jesus.

One way of reading what the original text actually says is simply that the Prince of Persia "stood before me", and that "I was there with the king of Persia". This prince/king was obviously the reason for Jesus' delay, but we shouldn't read that he's stronger than Jesus.

The issue

The mention of kingdoms of Persia and Greece, though, should alert us to what is happening. Those are the kingdoms involved in persecuting God's people. So the earthly battle has some kind of heavenly counterpart. This raises more questions than it answers but it means there's more going on than political rulers following their ambitions and God's people getting squashed on the way. There is also a spiritual battle being fought.

---

time out   Reflect on the following:

"Put on the full armour of God so that you can take your stand against the devil's schemes. For our struggle is not against flesh and blood, but against the rulers, against the authorities, against the powers of this dark world and against the spiritual forces of evil in the heavenly realms." (Ephesians 6 v 11-12)

Trouble and strife

▶ **Reading:** Psalm 141   **Sunday** 6 November

*I*t's crisis time for David again. But spot the strange requests as you…

▶ **Read Psalm 141**

Provoked…

❓ *How desperate is David (v 1-2)?*

❓ *But, strangely, what is he chiefly concerned about?*

Curiously, in the face of great provocation, David pleads with God for self-control. He is desperate not to retaliate with vicious words (v 3), or to get involved in his opponents' tactics (v 4)—but only to be remembered for speaking with gracious words (v 6).

> *apply*
>
> So let's admit it. Despite the calm exterior, we're often boiling with rage inside, thinking about how we're going to "get them back" or imagining cruel and unusual punishments for those who rub us up the wrong way. If you're anything like me, then you are particularly vulnerable to this kind of thinking when you are behind the wheel of the car…
>
> Perhaps it's time to take a leaf from David's book, and pray v 3-5…

… but protected

Why is it that David can behave so sensibly, humbly and spiritually, when his bones are crying out for revenge?

❓ *See the answers in v 6-8?*

He has learned to leave judgment in the hands of the one just Judge, trusting that He will vindicate His chosen one…

❓ *How about you?*

> *time out*
>
> Although this psalm is written by David, it is also the song of great David's greater son, who supremely showed self control before His false accusers, and entrusted Himself, life, body and soul to the One who could vindicate Him.
>
> **Compare Luke 23 v 8-9 with v 3-4; and Luke 23 v 47 with 6b.**

The compassionate touch

Reading: Daniel 10 v 15 – 11 v 1   **Monday** 7 November

W e're almost at the interpretation but there's more of a hold up as Daniel can't handle this experience.

The need for strength

▶ **Read Daniel 10 v 15-19**

❓ *What happens to Daniel in these verses?*

❓ *How would you describe Jesus' attitude?*

Daniel is left speechless by this vision (having collapsed once before—**see v 9**). A touch from Jesus strengthens him enough to be able to speak, but only enough to say that he can't handle it, it's too much for him.

So another touch gives strength and words of comfort and reassurance are spoken—and these very words give strength (**see v 19**). Daniel can finally say: "Speak, my Lord, since you have given me strength".

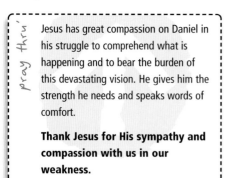

pray thru' Jesus has great compassion on Daniel in his struggle to comprehend what is happening and to bear the burden of this devastating vision. He gives him the strength he needs and speaks words of comfort.

Thank Jesus for His sympathy and compassion with us in our weakness.

The Book of Truth

▶ **Read 10 v 20 – 11 v 1**

❓ *Why has Jesus come to Daniel?*

❓ *What ideas does this "Book of Truth" raise?*

Jesus has come to explain what will happen to Daniel's people in the future (v 14); which is what is written in this Book of Truth. This gives the idea that God has a book containing all the events that are to happen. So they are all under His sovereign control.

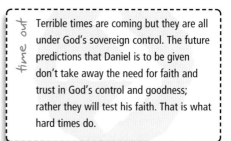

time out Terrible times are coming but they are all under God's sovereign control. The future predictions that Daniel is to be given don't take away the need for faith and trust in God's control and goodness; rather they will test his faith. That is what hard times do.

The future unveiled (part 1)

▶ **Reading:** Daniel 11 v 2-20   **Tuesday** 8 November

It's time to hear the vision itself as Jesus explains what will happen in the future. It's a story of politics and power in the ancient world. This doesn't immediately make for a gripping read, but God knows what He's doing in telling Daniel this stuff.

Power and politics

As in previous chapters, this gives an overview of political events following Daniel's time.

▶ **Read Daniel 11 v 2-20** using the notes below to help make sense

Verses 2-4: After ending the Persian kingdom, the Greek kingdom begins, whose "mighty king" is Alexander the Great. After him, his kingdom is divided into four.

Verses 5-13: These describe a series of alliances and wars between the "king of the south", which is Egypt, and the "king of the north", which is Syria. This is of relevance because between these two superpowers of the day is Israel—and God's people have returned after the exile.

Verses 14-20: The struggle between the north and south continues but now includes a reference to the involvement of Jewish people (v 14) and the "Beautiful Land" or Israel (v 16).

❓ What did you notice in these verses about people's motivations and attitudes?

❓ How does this fit with all these events being predicted by God?

This section includes repeated references to the ambition and desires of the kings involved. We read that someone will "do as he pleases" or was "filled with pride"; we read that people try to make alliances through marriage; we read of plans succeeding and plans failing. In other words, we read of all the normal stuff of political life that was swirling round Israel.

And yet this is all predicted fulfilment of what is written in God's Book of Truth (**see 10 v 21**). Here is divine sovereignty and human freedom side by side. This is what we've seen throughout Daniel: political leaders make their choices and yet only under God's sovereign hand.

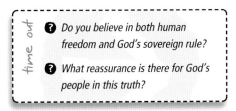

time out

❓ Do you believe in both human freedom and God's sovereign rule?

❓ What reassurance is there for God's people in this truth?

The contemptible ruler

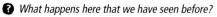

W e've seen some of the political movements and battles. Now we focus in once again on a specific ruler.

▶ **Read Daniel 11 v 21-24**

❓ *What's the general sense you are given about this ruler?*

Once again this matches Antiochus Epiphanes, who was a scheming but successful ruler. Some of the details are unclear but many of them can be matched to what we know of his rule eg: the prince of the covenant being destroyed (v 22) is probably the removal and later murder of the high priest in Jerusalem.

▶ **Read v 25-30**

This describes ongoing battles between the king of the north (Antiochus) and the king of the south (Egypt).

❓ *What new group appears in the narrative?*

❓ *What does the king of the north do to them?*

Once again we can match this up with historical records eg: the kings did have a conference marked by mutual deceit (v 27). But the new focus is on the king of the north's treatment of God's people— the "holy covenant". His heart is set against them (v 28), and after a later war, which he loses, he vents his fury against them.

He goes on to show favour to those Jews who will forsake the covenant (v 30).

▶ **Read 31-32**

❓ *What happens here that we have seen before?*

❓ *How are those who resist described?*

This is the moment where the king of the north brings a halt to the temple sacrifices and then desecrates the temple in Jerusalem (**see 7 v 25; 8 v 12-13**). Some of God's people give in to the pressure (v 32), but there are those who resist and stand firm. They are "those who know their God".

❓ *Given what we've learned from Daniel, why is this phrase used of these people?*

Remember the theme of the book: *God remains the true God so stay faithful to Him.* Those who know God know He's worth being faithful to.

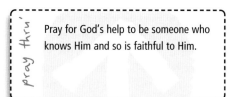

pray thru'

Pray for God's help to be someone who knows Him and so is faithful to Him.

Those who are wise

▶ **Reading:** Daniel 11 v 33-35   **Thursday** 10 November

We have begun to see those who stood firm and stayed faithful to God under persecution. We read more about them today.

Being faithful

▶ **Read Daniel 11 v 34-35**

❓ How is this faithful group now described?

❓ What may happen to them?

This group is called "wise". They are those who stay faithful to God themselves and teach others to do so as well. There will be moments when they receive "a little help" through people joining their cause, but many of them will only be fair-weather friends.

The point is that the decision of this group to remain faithful may not look very wise to an outsider: their faithfulness may cost them their possessions or their lives. But because God is the true God, staying faithful to Him is always the wise thing to do. We've learned that through Daniel—here's the sobering application of it. **Stay faithful no matter what.**

A similar point is made in the face of persecution in Revelation:
"If anyone is to go into captivity, into captivity he will go. If anyone is to be killed with the sword, with the sword he will be killed. This calls for patient endurance and faithfulness on the part of the saints."
(**Revelation 13 v 10**)

Being refined

▶ **Read v 35**

❓ What is God's purpose for His people in these hard times?

Persecution purifies the church. It is a sobering truth but a truth nonetheless. Peter says the same thing to his readers: "...though now for a little while you may have had to suffer grief in all kinds of trials. These have come so that your faith—of greater worth than gold, which perishes even though refined by fire—may be proved genuine and may result in praise, glory and honour when Jesus Christ is revealed."
(**1 Peter 1 v 6-7**)

> *pray thru'* Pray you will be "wise" in remaining faithful to God even when it looks like it is foolish—and that your faith will be refined as a result.

The king who exalts himself

▶ **Reading:** Daniel 11 v 36-45   **Friday** 11 November

W e now see the last days of this specific ruler who persecutes God's people. We start to see more of his attitude and, as a result, how sinister he is.

The exaltation

▶ **Read Daniel 11 v 36-39**

❓ *What sort of attitudes does this king start to show?*

❓ *What sort of things does he start to do?*

Again this section can be matched with some details from history (although not all of it is clear). For example, Antiochus printed coins which proclaimed himself as "god". The key issue here is his incredible arrogance and pride—exalting himself above all gods.

Once again we are talking about a historical figure, but we are also talking about a pattern of those who oppose God and His people. For example, in 2 Thessalonians we read of a very similar character who *"will oppose and will exalt himself over everything that is called God or is worshipped, so that he sets himself up in God's temple, proclaiming himself to be God"* (**2 Thessalonians 2 v 4**).

This leads us to the difficult issue of the antichrist (**see 1 John 2 v 18, 22**). What is clear is that this opposition from Antiochus is repeated through history and, in that sense, there are many antichrists—as we saw earlier, the pattern

is repeated. What is debated is whether there will be a final figure at the end of time who is the pinnacle of such evil opposition and hence is *the* antichrist.

The end

▶ **Read v 40-45**

❓ *What will finally happen to this king?*

❓ *What overall impression of him are we left with?*

There are more battles and victories but this is the "time of the end"—that is, the end of the time of this king and his persecuting rule. He will finish his rule in a characteristic way: with "great rage to destroy and annihilate many" (v 44). His final battle place is significant: between the sea, where the beast came from, and the holy mountain, where God reigns in Jerusalem.

> *time out*
>
> ❓ *How should we feel knowing such evil is allowed to devastate God's world, and yet that He will bring it to an end?*

Reviewing the battles

▶ **Reading:** Daniel 10 – 11   **Saturday** 12 November

Before we move into the final chapter of Daniel, it's worth pulling some threads together of what we've seen over the last chapters.

Review

❓ *What have been the central themes in Daniel's last vision?*

❓ *Why do you think there has been so much focus on one ruler?*

We've seen a huge amount of prophecy of political and military movement in the ancient world. But the focus is not what you'll find in the history books. Significant leaders like Alexander the Great have been mentioned, but only in a few verses, while Antiochus has taken up pages—even though internationally he wasn't a big deal.

The reason of course is that he was a big deal to God's people. Previous empires held little threat for the returned exiles in Israel and the recently rebuilt temple in Jerusalem. But after some years of stability back in the land, Antiochus appears and everything seems to be threatened again.

Consider

❓ *What do you think God's purpose is in telling His people these details beforehand?*

❓ *Why do you think it has been presented in so much detail?*

When Antiochus appeared and began his rampage, and when the temple was finally desecrated, God's people could easily have thought that God was angry with them again. They could have thought this was another exile just like the one under Nebuchadnezzar. They could have lost all hope.

But that's not the truth of the situation and so God gives this prophecy to prepare people for the hard times ahead. He shows He knows every detail of what will happen; it is all in the Book of Truth (**see 10 v 21**).

---

time out

"Prophecy never takes away the need for faith, rather it is given to encourage and strengthen faith" (Robert Fyall).

❓ *How does this section of Daniel show this to be true?*

Dave in the cave

▶ **Reading:** Psalm 142   **Sunday** 13 November

This psalm was written before David became king. At this point he was hiding out, on the run from Saul. God had told Saul that David would be king in his place one day. Saul, wild with jealousy, tried to kill David; hence the hideout.

▶ **Read Psalm 142**

Abandoned by everyone

❓ *How was David feeling (v 1-4)?*

Distress and loneliness (you've been abandoned, nobody cares about you, or understands the trouble you're in) are normal reactions to have in times of trouble. These feelings are not wrong, but what they lead to could be...

❓ *But what was David's reaction in his dire distress (v 2)?*

❓ *How is this an example to you when times are tough?*

❓ *How do you tend to react instead?*

Notice what gives David his great confidence (v 3a).

❓ *What else do we learn about David's situation (v 3b-4)?*

❓ *What did he tell God (v 5)?*

David knew he was abandoned by others (worse, opposed by them)—but not abandoned by God. He knew God was both his "refuge" (a place to escape to for safety) and his "portion" (his satisfaction).

❓ *Did David bottle up his emotions (v 6)?*

❓ *What did David admit about himself?*

❓ *Why did David want to be rescued (v 7)?*

❓ *Why was he sure he would be?*

By the time he had finished his prayer session, David was full of assurance. He knew God could work deliverance, and restore freedom and thankfulness, and the chance to meet God's people again.

apply

We've tended to focus on applying these psalms to ourselves. This time, let's think how we can apply it to others. You're drinking coffee after church and chatting with people. In response to "How are you?" you get the usual "Oh, fine thanks". But something tells you that there is more to be told.

❓ *How would you take the conversation on, and what would you encourage the person to do from this psalm?*

Shining like stars

W e've seen the end of the rule of Antiochus; now we jump ahead to the final end.

The final rescue

▶ **Read Daniel 12 v 1**

❓ *List the main events that are described here.*

The main events

❓ *What is the role of Michael in these verses?*

Michael is seen here as the protector of God's people. He will arise at a moment of great conflict, presumably to protect God's people so that they will "be delivered"'. The security of God's people is shown in that their names are "written in the book" (**see Revelation 20 v 11-15**). Here is the final rescue of God's people.

The final destination

▶ **Read v 2-4**

❓ *What great event is pictured here?*

❓ *What are the destinations spoken of?*

This is a picture of the general resurrection at the end of time (**see John 5 v 28-29**) where everyone stands before God. There are two destinations—everlasting life or everlasting contempt. At the end of time all of humanity will be divided into these two groups.

The challenge to Daniel's readers is to be part of the group who are "wise" (remember that phrase from chapter 11 v 33). Those who are wise are faithful to God and lead others to righteousness. Their future is that of shining like stars—a picture of vindication and glory.

time out

❓ *Given this comes after a picture of terrible suffering, how would this encourage God's people to faithfulness?*

We are told constantly, throughout the Bible, to stay faithful to God, and it will be worth it in the end. Resurrection and judgment day will put all of the pleasures or pains of life into perspective.

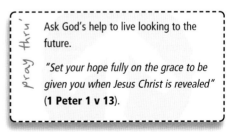

pray thru'

Ask God's help to live looking to the future.

"Set your hope fully on the grace to be given you when Jesus Christ is revealed" (**1 Peter 1 v 13**).

The end of the vision

W e come to the end of Daniel's last vision. Once again the question of timing is raised— but the answer is less about timing and more about trust.

How long

▶ **Read Daniel 12 v 5-7**

❓ What question is being asked?

❓ How is it answered, and in what manner?

The question asks how long it will be before all the astonishing events of chapters 11 and 12 will occur. The answer is given as a formal oath, showing utter certainty.

The length of time is the same as we saw earlier—three and a half (**see chapter 7 v 25**). We saw that this was both the approximate time (in years) that the persecution of God's people lasted, but that it also became a number symbolic of a time of persecution.

The time comes to an end when God's people are "finally broken". This is similar to the answer in Revelation when the martyrs ask: "How long?" and the answer is: when the number of Christians to be killed is completed (**Revelation 6 v 11**).

Go your way

▶ **Read v 8-13**

❓ What further details of timing are given?

❓ What are we told will happen during this time?

❓ What is Daniel told to do?

There's more detail on timing—again referring to the moment Antiochus stops the sacrifices and desecrates the temple. The point seems to be that you should wait faithfully until a time after that.

The focus is that God has spoken and it is decided—the words are closed up and sealed or authenticated. Many will be purified through the suffering to come, as we've seen earlier (11 v 35); and at the same time, those who are wicked will continue in their wicked ways. The call is again to be wise and so to understand what is happening; and so to trust God and live for Him.

So Daniel should simply "go his way". In other words, Daniel himself should live his life faithfully looking forward to his "allotted inheritance".

> *pray thru*
> Pray that you will be wise and "go your way", living for God in the light of His revelation.

Lessons from Daniel

▶ **Reading:** Daniel   **Wednesday** 16 November

W e'll finish our series with a study that summarises some of the lessons we've been learning from the wonderful book of Daniel. Remember the theme of the book has been: **God remains the true God so stay faithful to Him.**

God

❓ *What are some of the lessons you've learned about God?*

About God

You might like to look at **Daniel 2 v 20-23** and **4 v 34-35**.

God's kingdom

❓ *What have you learned about God's kingdom coming?*

About God's kingdom coming

You might like to look at **Daniel 2 v 44-45** and **7 v 13-14**.

Living for God

❓ *What have you learned about living for God under pressure?*

About living for God under pressure

You might like to look at **Daniel 1 v 8; 3 v 17-18; 11 v 32-33**.

The future for God's people

❓ *What have you learned about the future for God's people, which encourages faithfulness now?*

About the future for God's people

You might like to look at **Daniel 7 v 26-27** and **12 v 2-3**.

pray thru
Pray through the most significant lessons from Daniel for you.

1 Timothy: Doing church

Pastoring a church is a difficult business. Being part of a church is often not easy either. That's why the letter of 1 Timothy is gold-dust: because it's a "how-to" manual for a young pastor and his church. It will teach us how to pray for our church leaders; and it will teach us how to be productive church members.

▶ Read 1 Timothy 1 v 1-2

Notice the close father-son relationship between God's apostle Paul and Timothy.

Loving doctrine

▶ Read v 3-7

Timothy is leading the church in Ephesus (v 3). But he's young (4 v 12), and he's facing problems within the congregation.

❓ *What does Timothy need to do (v 3)?*

The "myths and endless genealogies" (v 4) is probably a reference to adding to the Old Testament. These teachers seem to have been going beyond what Scripture says; and then devoting themselves to what they'd added.

❓ *What's the outcome of false doctrine (v 4)?*

❓ *What is the aim of opposing it (v 5)?*

Good doctrine matters: but it's not an end in itself. Knowing the truth about God safeguards a congregation's hearts, conscience and faith.

False doctrine matters, too. It's easy to be swayed by confidence (v 7); but we need to look at the consequences and not the

delivery. Where there is controversy, there will usually be false doctrine (v 4).

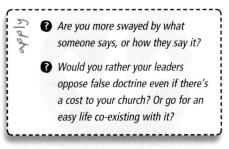

apply

❓ Are you more swayed by what someone says, or how they say it?

❓ Would you rather your leaders oppose false doctrine even if there's a cost to your church? Or go for an easy life co-existing with it?

Using law

▶ Read v 8-11

We need to use God's law properly (v 8).

❓ *Who is it not for (v 9)? Who is it for (v 9-10)?*

One function of the law is to show us we are not "righteous". We are the type of people Paul's talking about in v 9b-10a. The right use of the law is not to make us proud, nor allow us to look clever (like the false teachers, v 7), but to show us our need for Christ (see **Galatians 3 v 24**).

But once we've trusted in "the glorious gospel of the blessed God" (v 11), the law has another function: to show us how to live as God's people. So we need church leaders to teach us "sound doctrine" (v 11), that is in line with the gospel.

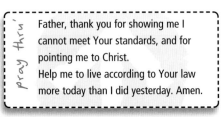

pray thru

Father, thank you for showing me I cannot meet Your standards, and for pointing me to Christ.
Help me to live according to Your law more today than I did yesterday. Amen.

Deserves full acceptance

▶ **Reading:** 1 Timothy 1 v 12-20   **Friday** 18 November

Today's study contains one of the most startling, and scintillating, statements anywhere in Scripture.

Who I was

▶ **Read 1 Timothy 1 v 12-15**

❓ How does Paul describe himself before he became a Christian (v 12-14)?

❓ How does he still view himself, even after all these years of being an apostle (v 15)?

What He did

❓ What has Jesus done (v 15)?

❓ What is both startling and scintillating about this fact?

❓ Why do we need to be able to say the second part of this "trustworthy saying" before we can appreciate the first part?

This is the gospel message: that we are more wicked than we could ever realise, and in more eternal trouble than we could ever imagine—and yet we are more loved, with a future more wonderful, than we could ever have dared hope.

What we do

▶ **Read verses 16-20**

❓ What is Paul doing in verse 17? Why is this the right response to the truth of verse 15?

In the past, Timothy had clearly been spoken of by other Christians as someone called into church ministry (v 18). And this letter is Paul's "instruction" to him as to how to fulfil those "prophecies" made about him.

❓ How does Paul sum up what Timothy is to do (end of v 18)?

❓ How can he do this (v 19)?

The Christian life, and especially Christian leadership, is a fight, a struggle. But struggling on is far better than being shipwrecked, which is what happens when we reject our conscience (v19). This happens to real people (v 20), who end up having to be excommunicated (that's what Paul's phrase in v 20 means) in the hope that this will shock them into returning to Christ.

pray thru Spend some time speaking to Christ Jesus now.
Begin with the second half of Paul's trustworthy saying, and confess your own sinfulness to the Lord.
Then take the first half of that saying to prompt you to praise Christ for coming to save you—even you!

apply ❓ Is there any way in which you're ignoring what your conscience is telling you? Listen to it now: ask God's forgiveness (remember v 15!), and then get on with living in line with what you know to be right.

Verse 15 is a stunning verse! Why not memorise it now and carry it with you always?

This is good

G od sent His Son into the world to save sinners (1 v 15) so they can receive eternal life (v 16). What does He want us to do with that life during our time on earth?

▶ **Read 1 Timothy 2 v 1-7**

Prayer

Notice the "then" in verse 1. Paul's words today link back to what he's just said about struggling on in the faith and never shipwrecking it (1 v 19-20).

❓ *What does Paul "urge" first of all (v 1)?*

❓ *Who is this to be done for in particular (v 2)?*

❓ *When we pray for them, what are we asking for (v 2)?*

❓ *Why is this "good"?*
- verse 3
- verse 4

Paul's logic is: if authorities maintain peace... we can get on with living clear Christian lives... and in such conditions others are most likely to hear and see "the truth", and be saved... which pleases God. So, we should get praying!

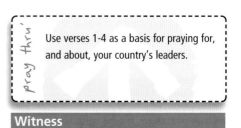

pray thru' Use verses 1-4 as a basis for praying for, and about, your country's leaders.

Witness

Our aim should be that all people "come to a knowledge of the truth" (v 4).

❓ *Why?*
- *v 3-4*
- *v 5*

Jesus is able to stand between God and us, bringing us into relationship with each other.

❓ *What has Jesus done in the past that enables Him to do this now (v 6)?*

❓ *Why is the job that Paul has been given (v 7) therefore of crucial importance?*

We are not apostles, as Paul was. But we can be "heralds", telling those around us that there is only one God, and only one way to be brought into relationship with Him—through faith in Christ Jesus. And we can be "teachers", telling those who already know Jesus more about Him.

time out It's easy to be negative or cross about our rulers, and to think today's governments are particularly ungodly. But the Roman Emperor when Paul wrote to Timothy was Nero, who was about to start burning Christians alive. If Christians then could pray positively for and about their leaders, then we certainly can.

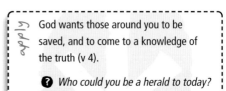

apply God wants those around you to be saved, and to come to a knowledge of the truth (v 4).

❓ *Who could you be a herald to today?*

Men, women and church

Reading: 1 Timothy 2 v 8-15   **Sunday** 20 November

These verses are not easy! They are tricky to understand, can be tricky to accept, and are often tricky to apply.

> **pray thru'**
> Thank God that "the words of the LORD are flawless" (Psalm 12 v 6). Ask Him to help you to understand what He's saying; to accept it; and to see how it applies in your life and your church.

Pattern

Read Genesis 1 v 27, 2 v 18-22

? What does 1 v 27 tell us about both men and women?

Verse 27 shows that men and women are *equal*, and *valuable*, to God. But men and women are *different*. Man needs woman (2 v 18): woman is made for man (v 21). Man is made to rule (so he has authority to name the animals, v 19-20); woman is made to help and support him as he does.

Principles

Read 1 Timothy 2 v 8-15

? What are men to do (v 8)?

All too often men rely on themselves, not God; or they speak to God while failing to be at peace with those around them. Men need to pray, and pray properly.

? What are women to do (v 9)?

? What is "beauty" in God's eyes (v 10)?

Christian women shouldn't dress to impress (otherwise instead of focusing on prayer, men will focus on them!). Equally, Christian men need to notice a girl's good deeds more than they notice her figure. A challenge for both sexes!

? What should women do (v 11)? What shouldn't they do (v 12)?

In v 13-14, Paul gives two reasons for what he says. The first (v 13) refers to the created pattern we saw in Genesis 1–2.

The second (v 14) is a Genesis 3 reason. In listening to the serpent, the woman acted as ruler rather than helper, making the decision to sin without even referring to her husband. When we step out of the pattern God created us to live in, we reject God.

There are two ways of reading verse 15:

• A woman who had the unique privilege of giving birth to our Saviour, Jesus.

• Women get to continue the human race through childbirth, and to bring their children up knowing God.

Practice

? Looking over verses 11-12, how do you think these verses should apply in your church?

The principles here are clear: women are not to teach with authority over men. But in practice, Christians who love God's word will have a variety of ways of applying these truths in their church settings. We need to pray that men take up their responsibility to lead; and that women support them as they do.

The leading question

W*hat should be on the CV or résumé of a church leader?*

▶ **Read 1 Timothy 3 v 1-7**

Leadership: the task

In verse 1, Paul talks about an "overseer". Traditionally this has been translated "bishop"; but Paul seems to have in mind anyone who is in authority over a church. The term "overseer" applies as much to a pastor or teacher in an individual church as it does to someone who has oversight of a group of congregations.

❓ *What does Paul say about the task of being an "overseer" (v 1)?*

This letter gives us an idea of how pastors should be chosen:

- We've already seen that "prophecies" were made about Timothy as a leader (1 v 18): there needs to be a sense that God is calling an individual to teaching leadership.

- In 4 v 14, Paul will talk about the time "the body of elders laid their hands on" Timothy: there needs to be public affirmation from the wisest, older members of a congregation that their church recognises an individual as called to be leader.

- In 3 v 1, Paul is referring to an inner desire to take on the "noble" task of oversight: a pastor needs to have set their heart on serving in this privileged, though difficult, way.

Leadership: the type

❓ *Pick out the fourteen "qualifications" Paul says an overseer needs (v 2-7).*

❓ *For each of these, think about why that qualification is so important for an overseer.*

❓ *What are the dangers Paul picks out:*
- *in v 6?*
- *in v 7?*

These are two separate dangers. In verse 6, Paul is thinking about a pastor becoming like the devil: proud, and so rebellious, and so facing judgment. In verse 7, the danger is a pastor falling into the "devil's trap" of having a bad reputation among the wider community, so that people don't take Christ seriously.

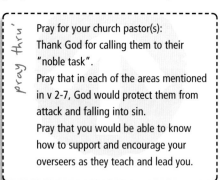

pray thru'

Pray for your church pastor(s): Thank God for calling them to their "noble task". Pray that in each of the areas mentioned in v 2-7, God would protect them from attack and falling into sin. Pray that you would be able to know how to support and encourage your overseers as they teach and lead you.

What a workplace!

▶ **Reading:** 1 Timothy 3 v 8-16   **Tuesday** 22 November

Paul now turns to list the qualifications for "deacons". Then he reminds Timothy, and us, why it is that leading a church is noble, and having the right leaders is vital.

The deacons and their wives

▶ **Read 1 Timothy 3 v 8-13**

It's unclear exactly what a "deacon" is, and does. But it seems they were people ("men" in v 8 isn't in the original Greek) who supported the overseers, both in serving but also in teaching (v 9 suggests they were expected to teach "the faith").

❓ *What qualifications does Paul set out for deacons (v 8-10, 12-13)?*

❓ *What about their wives (v 11)?*

This is a great reminder that, for church leaders who are married, ministry is a partnership. The wife of an overseer or deacon can double their ministry; equally, they can halve it. It is not easy being a church leader; but perhaps it is even harder being their wife!

pray thru
Pray for the wives (or husbands) of anyone in a leadership position in your church. Use verse 11 to shape your prayers.

The workplace

▶ **Read 1 Timothy 3 v 14-16**

❓ *How does Paul describe the church (v 15)?*

❓ *So, why is it vital to have the right people leading it?*

❓ *And why is it a "noble" (v 1) thing to be able to work there?*

time out
Read Ephesians 2 v 19-22.

❓ *What does this description of church, written by the same man to the same congregation, add to the picture in 1 Timothy 3?*

In Ephesians 2 v 20, the "foundation" of the church is the "apostles and prophets" —the truths contained in the Old and New Testaments. In 1 Timothy 3 v 15, the church is the "foundation of the truth". So which way round is it?! In fact, both are true. The church depends on the truth as revealed in Scripture for its existence; the church proclaims that truth, and is the foundation of it, in its mission. Without the truth, there will be no church; without the church, the truth will not be heard.

When Paul talks about "mystery" in verse 16, he means a secret that has been revealed.

❓ *What is the content of the "mystery" that leads to "godliness" (v 16)?*

Notice that it's the truth about Jesus that is the foundation of godly living. The more we live according to the truths God has revealed, the more we'll live godly lives.

A forbidding problem

The church is founded on the truth that Jesus lived on earth and now reigns in glory. And the church announces that truth to the world so people can turn to Christ. But tragically, it's not all one-way traffic…

▶ **Read 1 Timothy 4 v 1-10**

Abandoning

❓ *What will some who call themselves Christians do (v 1)?*

❓ *What does verse 1 reveal is the reason why this happens?*

This is how evil spiritual forces have always worked. In the Garden of Eden, the devil adopted a tactic of deceit, convincing Eve to believe the lie that God did not want what was best for her; and that life without God would be better than life under His rule (**Genesis 3 v 1-7**).

But usually (and unlike with Eve), these deceptions don't come directly from their demonic source.

❓ *How do church members hear these deceits (v 2)?*

❓ *Why does this make them particularly difficult to spot, and so especially dangerous?*

Forbidding

❓ *What were these teachers saying (v 3)?*

❓ *Why is this wrong (v 3-4)?*

As we enjoy God's gifts in God's world as God's people, what He created is doubly "consecrated", or made good. Firstly, because He made it in the first place: secondly, because we're using it with thanks, acknowledging Him as the provider.

❓ *How should a minister like Timothy react to the real danger of false teaching (v 6-8)?*

> **apply**
>
> Many of us say "grace" before meals, thanking God for our food.
>
> ❓ *But do you give thanks to God, either in your heart or out loud, for every good thing He gives you throughout the day?*

> **time out**
>
> In a world which forbids nothing, and permits everything, it's easy for Christians to be deceived into running in the opposite direction, and forbidding what God created as good and wants us to enjoy. So, just because sex outside marriage is increasingly accepted, it does not mean Christians shouldn't talk about sex. Just because drunkenness is a misuse of what God has made, it does not mean that drinking alcohol is sinful.
>
> What else can we wrongly become forbidding over? Here are some (potentially provocative!) ideas: what people wear to church… political view… humour in services… modern music…

> **pray thru'**
>
> Pray for your church, that you would never be deceived by false teaching. Pray for your leaders, that they would keep your church founded on the truth.

The pastor's day job

▶ **Reading:** 1 Timothy 4 v 11 – 5 v 2   **Thursday** 24 November

Paul has already set out the qualifications of a church pastor. But how should Timothy conduct himself now that he is a pastor?

▶ **Read 1 Timothy 4 v 11 – 5 v 2**

Conduct

❓ *What should Timothy not do (v 12)?*

❓ *How can any church leader prevent people doing this, whatever the reason (v 12)?*

Work

❓ *What should Timothy's priorities for his church be (v 13)?*

❓ *Why is the word "devoted" so striking here?*

time out

What is your church "devoted" to? Sadly, some churches are not devoted to the Scriptures, and preachers prefer to ignore the bits which are unpopular or difficult.

But it's easy to err in the opposite direction, too. In verse 13 Paul talks about "the public reading of Scripture" before he mentions preaching. It's easy to think, and to give the impression, that what matters in the service is not the Bible reading but the preaching; that God can't speak except through the pastor!

❗ *Keep a Bible open during the preach, checking it's Bible-centred.*

❗ *Think about what God's saying while His word is read, rather than just waiting for the preacher to explain it.*

Growth

❓ *What should Timothy **not** do (v 14)?*

God gives us gifts; but we have to work at using them as well as we can.

❓ *What should Timothy do (v 15-16)?*

A good Christian teacher is someone who goes on being a humble Christian student.

Relationships

❓ *What does Paul tell us about how the Christian family should relate to each other (5 v 1-2)?*

apply

❓ *Do you regard the other members of your church as your family?*

❓ *Is there anything you need to change in how you treat those older and younger than you?*

Look back over this passage at the way Paul tells pastors to behave, and what he tells them to prioritise.

❓ *Is this what you notice and care about most in a pastor?*

❓ *Is this what you're praying for your pastor?*

pray thru'

Spend some time now praying for your pastor, using some or all of the aspects of ministry in these verses to shape your prayers.

Widows and the church

Being a widow is not easy. Widowhood always begins with one of the worst experiences life can bring. And widows often find themselves at the margins of society. But God describes Himself as a "defender of widows" (Psalm 68 v 5); and He wants His people to reflect His care.

Widows in need

▶ **Read 1 Timothy 5 v 3-8**

"Proper recognition" (v 3) means financial assistance as well as time and care.

❓ *Who has the primary responsibility to support a widow (v 4, 8)?*

❓ *What kind of widow does Paul want the church to support (v 5)?*

Sadly, the reality of being a widow (or widower) is all too often one of facing great financial hardship and the misery of complete loneliness.

But this must never be the case within a church. A Christian widow, who hopes and trusts in God (v 5), should be able to rely both on her biological family, and failing that her church family, for comfort; emotional, financial and spiritual.

> ❓ *Who in your church is in need of comfort? How could you sacrificially serve with your money and your time?*
>
> ❓ *Could you commit to praying for a few recently-bereaved people who are part of your church?*

Widows, older and younger

▶ **Read 1 Timothy 5 v 9-16**

The "list of widows" in verse 9 seems to be different to the "proper recognition" list of verses 3-8. It's likely that it refers to a group of widows who had committed to working for the church as the church supported them (a little like deacons).

❓ *What kind of widows were eligible (v 9-10)?*

❓ *Who wasn't to be considered (v 11)?*

Younger widows may well, in time, wish to remarry. But they will then break their "first pledge" (v 12)—to be devoted to working for their church. Also, it would be very easy to use their role simply to gossip (v 13). Better to remarry.

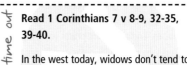

> *time out*
>
> **Read 1 Corinthians 7 v 8-9, 32-35, 39-40.**
>
> In the west today, widows don't tend to face the stark choice between working for the church or remarrying. Most have the opportunity to work for their living, and live as single women.
>
> ❓ *What does Paul say about how to live as a single woman (v 32-35)?*
>
> It's good to remain unmarried (v 40).
>
> ❓ *That said, what are the guidelines regarding remarriage (v 8-9, 39-40)?*
>
> ❓ *Whether your current role in life is unwanted or not, what opportunities does it give you to serve God?*

Pastors and bosses

▶ **Reading:** 1 Timothy 5 v 17 – 6 v 2   **Saturday** 26 November

How should we treat our church leaders? How should they treat each other? And how should we treat our bosses at work?

Elders

▶ **Read 1 Timothy 5 v 17-25**

❓ *What do elders who do their job properly deserve (v 17)?*

Verse 18 makes clear that Paul has financial pay in mind. But his instruction in v 17 means more than that. Church leadership can be a demoralising and debilitating job (as v 23 suggests). We can honour our church's leaders by encouraging them, supporting them and defending them, as well as by paying them.

❓ *When it comes to your pastor, could you make sure you always praise him four times as much as you criticise?*

❓ *How could you encourage your pastor this week?*

apply

In verses 19-25, Paul is talking to Timothy as the head elder about how he should treat the other church elders.

❓ *What situation is Paul talking about in v 19-20, and what is his advice?*

John Calvin, the sixteenth-century reformer, wrote that godly teachers "never avoid a thousand criticisms". Timothy mustn't even consider an accusation against a fellow-elder unless it's backed up by more than one witness. But,

Paul says in verse 20, he's not to go too far the other way either.

The "laying on of hands" in verse 22 refers to the selection of church leaders.

❓ *Why will following Paul's advice in v 22 help prevent the issues we looked at in v 19-20?*

This instruction is particularly important because first impressions can deceive. While sins which would disqualify a man from being an elder are sometimes obvious, others are deeply hidden (v 24). Many churches have been severely damaged by appointing men who looked good but turned out to have serious underlying weaknesses; not all have survived to tell the tale.

❓ *Why is it so important for pastors to remember verse 21?*

Bosses

▶ **Read 1 Timothy 6 v 1-2**

The Bible nowhere commends slavery: here Paul describes it as a "yoke". But it's still important to be godly in ungodly circumstances.

❓ *What principles can we take from these verses to apply to the modern-day workplace?*

---

pray thru'

Thank God for your pastor and elders. Pray that you'd be able to encourage them this week.

Thank God for your boss. Pray that your hard work would give you chances to witness to them about Christ.

Not drowning… but waving

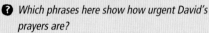

▶ Reading: Psalm 143   **Sunday** 27 November

J ust like Psalms 140-143, here's another psalm revealing King David's reaction to severe pressure. His situation in this one seems to be one step further: it's on the brink of engulfing him...

▶ Read Psalm 143

Watch the signs of change in David as he prays through his situation...

Under strain

▶ Read v 1-2

❓ What is David pleading for?

❓ What does he appeal to (v 1b, 2b)?

Shattered

▶ Read v 3-4

❓ What's happening to him (v 3a)?

❓ How does he feel (v 3b-4)?

Dry

▶ Read v 5-6

❓ What does David do (v 5)?

❓ Does this help (v 6)?

God's care seems to belong entirely in the past (v 5)—David seems to have no experience of His favour at the present time (v 6).

Longing

▶ Read v 7-8

❓ Which phrases here show how urgent David's prayers are?

❓ What does he appeal to (v 8b)?

Dedicating

▶ Read v 9-10

❓ What's he asking God here?

❓ What does it mean to "hide myself" in God?

Remembering

▶ Read v 11-12

❓ What are David's requests?

❓ What does he grip on to about God's character?

❓ How might this sustain him?

We're not told the outcome... just left with the reminder of God's unfailing love to His people (v 12).

> *apply*
>
> Dark times do come: of trouble, doubt, opposition, struggle... When they do, remember this: you're not the first. You're not alone. You're not without help. A crisis is also the opportunity to take hold of the faithful God.
>
> **❓** *Will you do so?*

Contented or coveting?

Why do you want to be godly? Why do you want to live God's way today (assuming you do!)?

Coins

▶ **Read 1 Timothy 6 v 3-5**

❓ *What kind of teacher does Paul describe in verse 3?*

The phrase at the end of that verse refers to the whole of the Bible: both the words our Lord said directly, and those He spoke indirectly through those who wrote the Scriptures.

❓ *What do their actions result in (v 4-5)?*

❓ *What is driving these people to be, or at least to appear, godly (v 5)?*

> *time out*
>
> **Read Romans 12 v 1.**
>
> There can be all kinds of unhealthy motivations for growing in godliness that lurk under the surface of our lives. It might not be to get rich, as it was for these teachers: but it could be because we like others noticing us, because we want to be given an important role in the church, or because we like feeling good about ourselves compared to others. We covet these things.
>
> It's very easy to make pursuit of godliness me-centred, not God-centred. Romans 12 v 1 pulls our godly living back to the only right motivations: as a response to God's mercy through the cross, and because it pleases our heavenly Father.

Contentment

▶ **Read 1 Timothy 6 v 6-10**

❓ *What does real, rightly-motivated godliness produce (v 6)?*

If we see godliness as a means to an end, we'll never find contentment—we'll always want more money, recognition, self-esteem. And however much of it we gain, one day we'll leave it behind (v 7).

But if we see knowing and serving God as an end in itself, we will be contented as we live each day for Him, looking forward to life beyond death with Him.

Coveting

Paul knows there are material necessities that we need in order to be content (v 8). But so often we forget to distinguish between what we *need* and what we *want*: between *necessities* and *luxuries*.

❓ *What's the problem with loving money (v 9-10)?*

❓ *What's the ultimate danger of loving money most, as though it were a god (v 10)?*

>
>
> ❓ *Be honest: why do you want to be godly? Are there, or could there easily be, any wrong motivations?*
>
> ❓ *Do you need to be less regretful about the things you don't have, and more thankful for what you do have?*
>
> **Re-read Romans 12 v 1** to motivate your godly living today.

But you…

*I*n signing off, Paul points Timothy back into his past, and forward into his future, as he urges him to keep living for Christ in the present.

Past and future

▶ **Read 1 Timothy 6 v 11-16**

❓ *What had Timothy done in the past (v 12)?*

We don't know if Timothy was baptised as an infant or adult. But clearly, on a particular day he publicly declared that he knew the truth about who Jesus is.

❓ *How did this follow Jesus' example (v 13)?*

❓ *What lies in the future (v 14-15)?*

Present

Every man and woman of God can look back to their baptism and/or conversion, and forward to Jesus' return.

❓ *How should we live in between those two dates?*
- *v 11*
- *v 12*

"Eternal life" isn't only about quantity, but *quality*. Christ's people are already living the life of the age to come, life under the Lord Jesus' rule. But we need to "take hold" of it; to embrace it and enjoy it more and more. The more we obey Paul's commands of verse 11, the more we'll live the life Jesus has rescued us for, the life God made us for, the life we want.

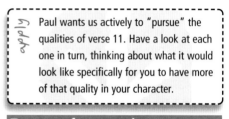

apply

Paul wants us actively to "pursue" the qualities of verse 11. Have a look at each one in turn, thinking about what it would look like specifically for you to have more of that quality in your character.

Treasure, future and present

▶ **Read 1 Timothy 6 v 17-21**

Paul wants wealthy people to "take hold of the life that is truly life"—eternal life with Christ—as well (v 19).

❓ *How can wealth prevent people from putting "their hope in God" (v 17)?*

❓ *How will the "man of God" use wealth?*

Rich or poor; single, married or widowed; young or old; church pastor or church member—anyone who follows Jesus has the greatest wealth of all. We have God's grace—God's undeserved gifts of mercy, of blessing, of "life that is truly life". We need to see all that we are and do in light of what God has done for us.

So Paul finishes by reminding Timothy that he has this grace (v 21). And the final "you" is plural—the encouragements, and the challenges, of this letter are for every man and woman of God, in all ages, including ours.

apply

❓ *From the book of 1 Timothy:*
- *what has most encouraged you?*
- *how have you been challenged?*
- *what specific changes in your attitude or actions are you making?*

ECCLESIASTES: A problem

▶ **Reading:** Ecclesiastes 1 v 1-2

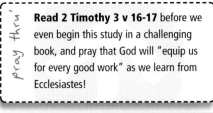

Read **2 Timothy 3 v 16-17** before we even begin this study in a challenging book, and pray that God will "equip us for every good work" as we learn from Ecclesiastes!

Making sense?

▶ **Read Ecclesiastes 1 v 1-2**

❓ *Who springs to mind as the author of this book?*

❓ *How do you react to verse 2?*

Our culture seems peculiarly obsessed with the "Public Inquiry". Whenever there is a disaster or a scandal, there is an immediate demand for answers. For all its faults, however, this obsession reveals a human conviction that "life should make sense" and that justice should prevail.

The book of Ecclesiastes is like a Public Inquiry. A wise man* seeks to provide answers to the apparent confusion of life. As we study this book we'll see the evidence and read his ongoing reflections. But we don't have to wait until the end for his conclusion. It's right here at the beginning: "Meaningless! … Everything is meaningless" (NIV). Other translations use such words as "vanity" (ESV), uselessness, or futility.

❓ *Do we too readily get sucked in to the general negativity of the world around us?*

Meaningless?

No wonder that Christians find this a difficult book! If we are telling people that Christ will give meaning to their lives, it doesn't help having a book in the Bible saying life is "meaningless". Could the verdict of Ecclesiastes be "ironic"—"Life *would* be empty without God"? The same word is used thirty-eight times throughout the book by the writer, a man with God in his life, and is repeated at the conclusion: "'Meaningless! Meaningless!' says the Teacher. 'Everything is meaningless!'" (12 v 8)

Are you ready to tackle this fascinating book?

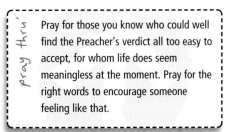

Pray for those you know who could well find the Preacher's verdict all too easy to accept, for whom life does seem meaningless at the moment. Pray for the right words to encourage someone feeling like that.

* **PS:** *The Hebrew word for the speaker in Ecclesiastes indicates "someone who addresses an assembly", so I'll call him the "Preacher".*

The Preacher's identity

No, "1 Kings" isn't a misprint! Let's look at the likely context of Ecclesiastes and at what life was like for God's people. 1 Kings 4 gives us a good idea of life at that time.

Read 1 Kings 4 v 20-34

❓ Would the word "meaningless" immediately spring to mind having read this passage?

One might be forgiven for thinking that Ecclesiastes was written in times of great trouble—compare the tone of Ecclesiastes with that of Lamentations, which really *does* come from such a time, during the Exile. Traditional biblical scholarship puts Ecclesiastes in the era of Solomon "son of David, king in Jerusalem" (**Ecclesiastes 1 v 1**). Ecclesiastes is not an inquiry into the circumstances that brought God's judgment on a guilty nation. Rather it is commenting on *ordinary* life, not the aftermath of disaster!

So what does **1 Kings 4 v 20** tell us? Solomon had brought the people of Judah and Israel to the point where they had "never had it so good". They were happy and prosperous, living in the land God had promised to Abraham (**see Genesis 12 v 1-3**), under the successor God had promised to David (**see 2 Samuel 7 v 12**)—a king to whom God had given unprecedented wisdom (**1 Kings 4 v 29**). Like Bob Geldof after the original *Live Aid* concert, the Preacher seems to ask: "Is that *it*?" Was this *really* the fulfillment of God's plans and purposes?

Count your blessings!

time out

Do you take the time to acknowledge *blessings* in your life, or are you too ready to complain and find fault?

Take a moment to count your blessings, and be thankful!

As we follow the Preacher's inquiry, we will find him asking: "What is the point of it all?" Perhaps you're a leader in industry, church or community? Perhaps you're "just" a housewife? We can find ourselves asking the same thing. Does it actually make any difference?

However…

apply

Read Colossians 3 v 17.

Challenged? Yes, I was! Make a positive decision today to do whatever it is you do "in the name of the Lord Jesus".

What goes around…

▶ Reading: Ecclesiastes 1 v 3-11　　　　　　**Friday** 2 December

The poet Edna St Vincent Millay was pretty close to the spirit of Ecclesiastes when she wrote: *"It's not true that life is one damn thing after another—it's one damned thing over and over".*

Here we go again…

▶ Read Ecclesiastes 1 v 3-11

? *What is your reaction to verse 8?*

? *Does it seem to sum things up for you?*

Ecclesiastes opens with something like "What goes around, comes around"—and round, and round, and round. The Preacher picks out three examples from the treadmill of nature: "the sun rises and … sets, and hurries back to where it rises" (v 5), "the wind blows … round and round … ever returning on its course" (v 6), and "to the place the streams come from, there they return again" (v 7).

Isn't it the same with daily chores? You cook, you eat, you wash up. Then you cook, you eat..! Not so bad when life's going well, but it's much harder to "keep on keeping on" when the compensations seem less obvious. At those times, things really become wearisome (v 8).

pray thru' Life is not always amazingly exciting. Pray for a godly attitude towards life's wearisome repetitions.

So, what's new?

The era of Solomon, for all its peace and prosperity, was not turning out to be as deeply satisfying as generations had longed for. There was "nothing new under the sun" (v 9) and it seemed like the old life recycled, and not even the hope of being remembered for posterity (v 11).

time out **?** *How can disappointment actually help us to see things God's way?*

pray thru' **Read Lamentations 3 v 22-23** (written during a time of great hardships) and compare this with what the Preacher sees. Pray that in whatever is your "daily grind", you can rejoice in God's mercies, "new every morning".

apply George Herbert (1593-1633) wrote in the hymn *Teach me, my God and King:*

*"A servant with this clause,
Makes drudgery divine.
Who sweeps a room as for thy laws,
Makes that, and the action, fine."*

What's it all about?

66

Read Ecclesiastes 1 v 12-18

❓ *What is the Preacher calling a "heavy burden"?*

❓ *How serious was the Preacher's inquiry?*

According to a letter to *The Times* by Valerie Eliot, the wife of the late T S Eliot, a London cabbie once said to her husband: "Only the other evening I picked up Bertrand Russell, and I said to him: 'Well, Lord Russell, what's it all about?' and, do you know, he couldn't tell me".

Russell was one of the most brilliant philosophers England ever produced. So the cab driver obviously thought he ought to have at least some idea of what it's all about! The same challenge, however, faced the Preacher in Ecclesiastes. Assuming the role of king over Jerusalem, and as someone who had received divine wisdom (v 16), he of all people should be able to answer the question: "What's it all about?"

An easy question to answer? On the contrary! The Preacher sees that it's a "heavy burden" (v 13) to be living with an endless cycle of repetition (v 9). So what answers come from the everyday business of life? Well, nothing obvious. In fact, just "chasing after the wind" (v 14)—a fruitless exercise, if you've ever tried it!

And there will always be aspects of life in a fallen world that remain mysterious— "What is twisted cannot be straightened; what is lacking cannot be counted" (v 15) because God, in His infinite wisdom, has chosen not to reveal the answers to all mankind's questions.

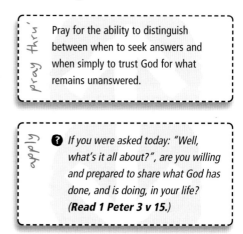

pray thru

Pray for the ability to distinguish between when to seek answers and when simply to trust God for what remains unanswered.

apply

❓ *If you were asked today: "Well, what's it all about?", are you willing and prepared to share what God has done, and is doing, in your life? (**Read 1 Peter 3 v 15.**)*

Jesus said: "Who of you by worrying can add a single hour to his life?" (**Matthew 6 v 27**). Since the answer is "None of you", aim today to put your trust completely in God rather than waste precious time worrying!

Past, present, future

*I*t's a psalm by King David. He's recalling God's help in subduing the enemies he faced—and looking to God for future help with great confidence. You'll get the idea as you **read Psalm 144**.

Past: thanks

▶ Read v 1-4

❓ *What thoughts have set David singing (v 1-2)?*

"Rock" combines (in the Bible) the ideas of strength, changelessness, refuge and provision. What a description of God...

Note He is both David's "loving God" and "fortress, stronghold" etc.

❓ *Why is it great that both are true?*

Get the shocking contrast between God and humans (v 3-4).

How amazing is it therefore that God acts the way He does!

Present: tense

▶ Read v 5-11

❓ *What's David's prayer in his new time of trouble (v 5-8)?*

❓ *What shows his confidence in God (v 9-11)?*

Future: hope

▶ Read v 10-15

❓ *What did David look forward to (v 12-14):*

    for his family?

    for the nation of God's people?

❓ *What does he remain sure of (v 15b)?*

And now...

This psalm has shown us...

... a king, given victory by God, who benefits his people.

Of course, we're pointed to the Lord Jesus Christ.

Those who trust in Jesus share in the benefits of His victory and look ahead to a glorious, eternal future.

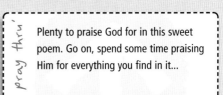

pray thru'   Plenty to praise God for in this sweet poem. Go on, spend some time praising Him for everything you find in it...

Empty pleasures

▶ **Reading:** Ecclesiastes 2 v 1-11

▶ Read Ecclesiastes 2 v 1-3

❓ *Do you sometimes find yourself going after material pleasures, maybe as a kind of escapism?*

❓ *Do you feel "satisfied" afterwards, or do you quickly realise the emptiness of "chasing after the wind"?*

"If it feels good, do it" has long been a prevailing philosophy of the western world: it is "natural" to do what feels good, and this appealing phrase makes total moral liberty sound like a profound choice.

So why is the Preacher willing to seriously try this? Because he's investigating whether "feeling good" might be an indication that something is good—so maybe we *ought* to seek pleasure because this is "what it's all about" for the short time we're here on earth, under heaven (ie: leaving God out of the picture, v 3). "Having a laugh" and a few drinks and indulging in worldly pleasures do not give meaning to life and certainly this isn't the purpose of life.

❓ *Do you have non-Christian friends for whom you are willing to commit to pray that they might see the emptiness of a life "chasing after the wind" without Christ—and that their hearts might be opened to accept the good news?*

Everything ventured, nothing gained

▶ Read 2 v 4 – 11

The Preacher now turns to the joys of creativity and building projects, and does find a genuine delight in the enterprises (v 10b), though when they are completed, they're found to be "meaningless, a chasing after the wind" (v 11). Once again, he is no nearer finding the answer.

By all means plan your party or put up your pergola. But don't imagine that with all your money, time, talent or effort you could produce something really "meaningful".

❓ *The media often feature examples of people who find meaning in their "dream scheme" or project. Should we share or avoid the same ambitions? What difference does "under the Son" thinking make?*

Thank God for the genuine pleasures in your life. Pray for His help to keep them in proper perspective.

The emptiness of wisdom

▶ **Reading:** Ecclesiastes 2 v 12-17   **Tuesday** 6 December

---

▶ **Read Ecclesiastes 2 v 12 - 17**

❓ *Which two opposites is the Preacher looking at here?*

❓ *What's his conclusion?*

So far the Preacher has drawn a blank. His wisdom has shown him that meaning, fulfilment and purpose are not to be found in pleasures—not even those of achievement available to a wise king with huge resources. But is there another possibility? What if the answer lies not in the *things* he is examining, but in the *means* by which he examines them—in wisdom (1 v 16-18). What if being wise is what it's all about? So the inquiry now re-focuses on wisdom—and also its opposites, namely madness and folly (v 12a).

Hitting a brick wall?

Obviously "wisdom is better than folly" (v 13a). That's as plain as daylight (v 13b)! But what of it? Wisdom itself is an utterly inadequate answer because the same fate overtakes both the wise and the foolish (v 14). Neither the wise man nor the fool will ultimately be remembered, and death comes to all equally (v 16). As George Bernard Shaw put it: "Death is the ultimate statistic; one out of one will die".

Here, it seems, the Preacher hits a brick wall. The very wisdom that apparently qualifies him to find answers actually betrays him. Yet, however hateful life seems (v 17), the wise cannot drop out of it, even though it is "chasing after the wind".

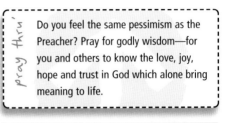

pray thru Do you feel the same pessimism as the Preacher? Pray for godly wisdom—for you and others to know the love, joy, hope and trust in God which alone bring meaning to life.

Got the right attitude?

▶ **Read Philippians 2 v 1 – 11**

To those who may feel discouraged, Paul urges a refocus. Rather than sink with the downward spiral of the Preacher's findings in Ecclesiastes, Paul exhorts us to look *out* (v 4) and look *up* (v 5) in this beautiful hymn of praise of our Lord.

pray thru In whatever situations we find ourselves, we have One against whom all our attitudes, actions and reactions must be measured (Philippians 2 v 5).

The emptiness of toil

▶ **Reading:** Ecclesiastes 2 v 17-23

▶ Read Ecclesiastes 2 v 17-23

The Preacher has realised that even this great gift—wisdom—does not satisfy. It has made him aware that there is no ultimate satisfaction in worldly achievements. Look at his conclusions (v 17).

❓ *Do you have days when you feel similarly?*

❓ *Do you turn your thoughts to prayer… or despair?*

You can't take it with you...

He hates his achievements because he must leave them behind, with no way of knowing whether he will leave them to a wise man or a fool (v 19). And the more he thinks about this, the worse it looks! Those great projects which held out such hopes earlier (v 4-8) now cause him despair (v 20).

> *time out*
> ❓ *Do you think "ski-ing" ("**S**pending the **K**ids' **I**nheritance") is such a bad idea?*
>
> ❓ *Is there anything in which you can invest your time, skills, efforts and money that **will** everlastingly survive you and the "fools" that may follow you?*

A Hard Day's Night?

❓ *Do you find you "take work home" with you (v 23)?*

❓ *Do you find yourself in sympathy with the Preacher's findings?*

By this stage, the Preacher's thoughts are in free-fall. All this labouring is "vanity and a great evil" (v 21b, ESV). Potentially worse than useless!

> *time out*
> ❓ *What kind of importance do you put on your work?*
>
> You may be clever and conscientious: your reports may be the best, your department the most successful, your company the fastest growing, your house the cleanest, your garden the neatest. But then someone else inherits it (v 21). Look up **1 Timothy 6 v 7** and ponder…

The Preacher started out confidently looking for the meaning of life. Instead, he finds himself plunging into despair. Can anything pull him out of it? (*Try to resist the temptation to look at tomorrow's reading!*)

> *pray thru'*
> Pray for wisdom about the way you are using your time and spending your money today. Pray that you can maintain an eternal perspective, a gospel perspective, in all that you do, so that ultimately it is not "meaningless".

The emptiness of despair

▶ **Reading:** Ecclesiastes 2 v 24-26   **Thursday** 8 December

Eat, drink and be merry?

▶ **Read Ecclesiastes 2 v 24-26**

❓ *What change of perspective do we read in these verses?*

❓ *According to the Preacher's observations, what can we not do without God?*

The Preacher has previously expressed despair precisely because of his wise perception of the folly of life. If we fail to find "what it's all about", we may be tempted to say that futility and despair themselves are the answer (*nihilism*).

The Preacher now has a different answer, which is neither despair nor delusion: "Wisdom, knowledge and happiness" which God gives (v 26). However meaningless it may seem, *work* is a gift from God (v 24) so it is right to find satisfaction in work.

❓ *But to **whom** does God give enjoyment?*

If we have relationship with God, our experience of life is transformed from drudgery to enjoyment. You might actually enjoy the washing up if it's an excuse to please or spend time alone with your Lord!

Silver service

▶ **Read Exodus 28 v 3; 31 v 3-4; 35 v 31**

❓ *What do these verses say to you about "work"?*

The first time the Bible refers to the Holy Spirit working in individuals, it is here in these artists and craftsmen who design and build the tabernacle, so that they are equipped to fulfil the particular task to which they have been called.

> *apply*
>
> ❓ *Can you think of skills, knowledge and areas of expertise that you have?*
>
> ❓ *How might you use them increasingly in the service of the Lord and for His glory?*

▶ **Read again Ecclesiastes 3 v 25-26**

❓ *What about those "without Him"?*

Notice that "without Him", satisfaction is out of reach (v 25). Everything adds up to meaningless drudgery, "chasing after the wind". Even worse, in their wearisome work the non-believer or atheist is unknowingly employed by the very God they deny, not for *their* benefit, but for *His* plans and the ultimate benefit of *His* people (v 26b).

> *pray thru'*
>
> Pray for those you know whose lives do reflect meaninglessness and weariness, and pray for opportunities to introduce them to the wonderful purposes of God.

A time for everything

▶ Read Ecclesiastes 3 v 1-9

❓ *How do you read these verses?*

- *That time is a tyrant and life is in a constant state of change over which we have no control? Or…*

- *That time is a blessing, and that this "poem" is a celebration of the variety of life?*

These are surely some of the most well-known verses in the Bible, popularised by the American folk-singer Pete Seeger in the 1960s. But very few read them in context. Far from being a piece of philosophical whimsy that provides us with the answer to life's questions, they summarise the Preacher's stark realisation that life doesn't contain the answer.

The message here is not a simple statement that there is "a time and a place for everything". Rather, this list of opposites is like a proverbial version of Sir Isaac Newton's *Third Law of Motion*: "For every action there is an equal and opposite reaction". Here the Preacher observes that for every reality of life there is an equal and opposite reality. So for birth, there is death (v 2a), for planting there is uprooting (v 2b), and so on. In the endless complexity of life, there is an appropriate occasion for every human event or activity—an unfolding pattern, exciting and God-given.

▶ Read verse 8 again

❓ *What is your reaction to this verse?*

▶ Read Psalms 31 v 6 and 139 v 21-22

❓ *What times and circumstances do you feel justify righteous anger?*

---

time out

In 1964, the Bachelors sang optimistically *I Believe*, "every time I hear a newborn baby cry, or touch a leaf, or see the sky".

❓ *But what should we believe when we see an old person with Alzheimer's in a nursing home, or hurricane clouds gathering that will devastate a community? Why are life's circumstances an unreliable guide to faith?*

---

pray thru'

Pray for those who may have lost their "faith" because disaster struck them or someone they cared about. Pray that they can look beyond the triumphs and disasters of this life to God and eternity, to gain hope and a right perspective.

God's gift

▶ Reading: Ecclesiastes 3 v 10-13   **Saturday** 10 December

▶ Read Ecclesiastes 3 v 10-13

❓ *What do you think the Preacher means in verse 11?*

❓ *What is the "gift of God" in verse 13?*

The "burden" (NIV) or "business" (ESV) God has given to mankind in v 10 has the sense of an "uphill task". Life can be a struggle, not just for survival, but a struggle to keep going when we realise that neither life nor our achievements are going to last.

Yet life is not all bleakness and despair (compare 2 v 24). Indeed, there are real moments of beauty to be enjoyed (3 v 11). We can look ahead, beyond the present, and know there is a future. We can look back in our history and understand the past, and yet we are also aware of our limitations (v 11b). And all this is God-given!

> *time out*
> Yuri Gagarin, the first man in space, reportedly said from orbit: "I don't see any God up here" (though, as someone later pointed out, he would have done if he'd opened the hatch). Why should we not be surprised Gagarin didn't "find God" out there?

Count your blessings!

So should we give up on exploring space, studying history or even indulging in our pastimes? Not at all! As the Preacher observes: "There is nothing better for men than to be happy and do good while they live" (v 13). The Preacher is not begrudging the enjoyment of life, but rather commending it.

▶ Read 8 v 15

It is a great gift of God when everyone has enough to eat and drink, and work which they enjoy. When the Preacher brings God and His blessings into the picture, our experience of life can be transformed from despair to delight. But those blessings are still not actually "what it's all about".

> *pray thru'*
> Pray for those who are "blinded by science" when it comes to God. Pray that their eyes will be opened to the limitations of human knowledge, and their need for God.

> *apply*
> God has given us *so* many things to enjoy. Have a nice day!

The world and the word

▶ **Reading:** Psalm 145

Before we read this terrific little psalm, write down five things that your non-Christian friends (we'll assume you've got some...) might say about God (He doesn't exist, He's out of touch, etc)

God is...
1.
2.
3.
4.
5.

▶ **Now read Psalm 145**

Excited...

▶ **Read v 1-7**

❓ *What specific things is David excited about?*

❓ *Which one strikes you the most?*

...about God...

▶ **Read v 8-16**

❓ *How is God described here?*

❓ *In what ways is He involved in the world?*

David spoke from his own experience. Christians nowadays should be able to say that they too have experienced the truths here.

❓ *Can you think of examples for yourself of the truths in v 8, 13b, 14, 16?*

...who is both great and near...

▶ **Read v 17-21**

❓ *What encouragements are there here?*

❓ *And what warnings?*

...so we should...

❓ *Now list all the responses that David says we, and others, should be making to this great God (v 1-8)...*

We should...

Notice that all those responses have to do with communication... talking to God and to others about how great He is.

...and also...

Now back (finally) to your friends' views.

❓ *How would you answer each point they have made?*

❓ *Why is it so important that you do (v 20)?*

> pray thru'
>
> The first step is to get praying: for your friends, and for your own knowledge of God and enthusiasm for Him. And pray for opportunities to share with them how great God is.

The "otherness" of God

So far, the Preacher's inquiry does not seem to be going that well. Far from discovering "what it's all about", he has merely seen that none of the usual things on which we expend so much energy reveal the answer. Even wisdom itself turns out to be "meaningless" if we look to it to provide the missing "meaning"!

Read Ecclesiastes 3 v 14-15

❓ Do you want to add "Amen" to those verses?

❓ According to these verses, what can all the "wisdom" and "toil" of chapter two add to the enduring work of God?

The Preacher, as a man of faith, knows that life is certainly "about" something. Specifically, *God* provides the element of permanence missing from human life and endeavours. *All* that *He* does endures *for ever*, without anything ever being taken away from it (v 14a). And that difference should evoke awe (v 14b, literally "so that they should *fear* before him"). Moreover, the past is not lost. On the contrary, as v 15 observes, "God will call the past to account".

---

pray thru'

Pray that today God will keep you from anything which you might not wish Him to remember.

Called to account...

Here the Preacher first sounds a note which modern theology often denies: God will one day bring *everything* to a future judgment, and He is able to do this precisely because *nothing* is lost to Him.

But how can God do this if all of us, wise and foolish, good and wicked, share the same fate in death—a realisation of which the Preacher is already aware (2 v 14)? The answer must be *there is something else*. But the Preacher is not yet in a position to say what it is! And so the inquiry continues...

Read 1 John 1 v 8 – 2 v 3

Thank God for Jesus!

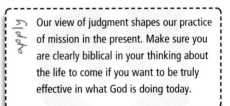

apply

Our view of judgment shapes our practice of mission in the present. Make sure you are clearly biblical in your thinking about the life to come if you want to be truly effective in what God is doing today.

God's justice in question?

God will one day call **all** things to account, so the Preacher concludes that there is an answer to the question: *"What's it all about?"*

Read Ecclesiastes 3 v 16-17

? *What reassurance does the Preacher find after his observations in verse 16?*

The Preacher sees rampant *injustice*. The ESV translation is good here: "in the place of justice even there was wickedness, and in the place of righteousness even there was wickedness". Justice and righteousness have long been established as twin characteristics of God. There is indeed a time "for every activity", and this includes a time for *judging*.

> *pray thru'*
>
> Pray for those caught up in situations of injustice, that they will not be tempted to doubt God.

From dust, to dust...

Read 3 v 18-22

? *Does the Preacher's thought of verse 18 shock you?*

The "test" seems to be that we cannot tell from *observation* that human beings are any different from the animals (v 18b, 19a). Both die the same way, both live the same way ("all have the same breath", 19b). Clearly (on the surface) we are no better off than beasts. Both we and they are living "dust" (v 20), and any

ideas about an afterlife are mere speculation (v 21). But if we see ourselves as "naked apes", then we will be ignorant of the coming judgment (v 17) and fail the ultimate test! We will continue *living* "meaninglessly", rather than *confronting* the "meaninglessness" of life.

Read Psalm 49

? *How do the Preacher's conclusions compare with the Psalmist's?*

> *apply*
>
> **?** *How do you find yourself reacting to the success of people who would seem to have no faith in, or even regard for, God?*
>
> **?** *If a non-believing friend was awarded a huge pay rise, how would you "congratulate" him or her?*
>
> **?** *How do you view your own personal "riches"?*

> *time out*
>
> **Read Genesis 1 v 27-30** and rejoice that God has made man unique—indeed, in His image—and we are each a living soul, responsible and accountable, who can have, in Christ, a wonderful future with Him to look forward to.

Oppression and ambition

▶ **Reading:** Ecclesiastes 4 v 1-4   **Wednesday** 14 December

---

▶ **Read Ecclesiastes 4 v 1**

❓ *Do you share the sympathetic grief of the Preacher at the plight of the oppressed in verse 1?*

> *pray thru'*
>
> Before we go any further today, pray for Christians caught up in oppression—from governments, or regimes, or inhumane working conditions.

Having begun to consider the issue of injustice (**Ecclesiastes 3 v 16**), the Preacher goes on to the question of the oppression that some inflict on others, and he simply sees *all* the oppression "under the sun" and that the oppressor has *power*. Who, then, can comfort the oppressed and deliver them?

> *time out*
>
> **Read 2 Corinthians 1 v 3-7** and think about how Paul praises:
>
> - the God and Father of our Lord Jesus Christ
> - the Father of compassion
> - the God of all comfort, who comforts us in all our troubles.

Better off dead?

▶ **Read 4 v 2-4**

Derek Kidner writes that: "There is nothing sadder in the whole book than the wistful glance in verses 2 and 3 at the dead and the unborn, who are spared the sight of so much anguish". The Preacher comes to a bleak conclusion indeed. Of course, most of us will reject this conclusion, but we're probably not currently being oppressed, are we?

> *time out*
>
> ❓ *Do you share the Preacher's sympathetic grief at the plight of the oppressed in our world?*
>
> ❓ *Is it inevitable that we accept this? What choices do you have that could affect them?*

Of course, not all oppression is extreme. Indeed, much oppression finds its origins in very mundane activities, particularly regarding "labour and achievement" (v 4). The key motivation being greed. So we accept our goods being made in China, in spite of the persecution of Christians there, because it is cheaper. And we *don't* ask questions about working conditions and wages paid to food producers in poorer countries, provided the price is right for us.

Economic realism? "This too is meaningless, a chasing after the wind" (v 4).

> *pray thru'*
>
> Pray for wisdom and courage in your dealings with the world.

To work, or not to work?

These days, economic activities are held up by politicians as the benchmark against which other decisions should be measured. But, as the Preacher has noted, these activities are motivated largely out of envy rather than love for others. They lead to oppression and injustice, as we simply ignore the impact on others of the goals we are pursuing.

▶ **Read Ecclesiastes v 5-6**

❓ *What does the Preacher seem to be advocating here?*

Is it then a godly response to withdraw from the economic sphere—simplify our lifestyle, give up all earthly labours and await the kingdom? The trouble is, we end up in dire poverty, needing the help of others! As the proverb in verse 5 right-ly says: "The *fool* folds his hands and ruins himself".

All work and no play?

But proverbs often come in apparently contradictory pairs. Just as "Too many cooks spoil the broth," so "Many hands make light work,"—and it takes *real* wisdom to know which applies. So, although it's true that economic indifference leads to ruin, equally, economic obsession leads to "toil and chasing after the wind" (v 6).

time out

❓ *Is there any point to working all the hours God sends so that you can enjoy life after you retire (if you live that long), when you could slow down a bit and enjoy life now? Wisdom or folly?*

❓ *What about gospel, missionary or church work? Do the same considerations apply?*

The work of God

▶ **Read John 6 v 25-29**

pray thru'

Pray that in whatever is "work" for you, your faith in Him will shine through.

Pray for those (maybe yourself) who work in an environment where the "work ethic" is everything but where godly wisdom is lacking.

apply

Think about your attitude to work (paid or unpaid). Are you in danger of ruining yourself like the fool, or working yourself to an early grave, "chasing after the wind"? It's OK to take a break—unless you are lazy, in which case, do some work!

The working fool

Reading: Ecclesiastes 4 v 7-8   **Friday** 16 December

The book of Proverbs is full of advice to the lazy fool. The best known is probably Proverbs 6 v 6 —"Go to the ant, you sluggard; consider its ways, and be wise!" The Preacher is not unaware of the problem of laziness, but he is more concerned with the question of **meaning**— what it is all about. This is probably not something that the lazy fool cares about. By contrast, the workaholic's driven-ness seems to provide the answer to the search for meaning.

The rat race

Read Ecclesiastes v 7-8

According to the Preacher, such work is an empty deception. The man in this example lacks nothing, yet he keeps on working to acquire even more wealth. Even he can see this is senseless, but he can't stop himself!

> *apply*
>
> **Read 1 Timothy 5 v 8 and Ephesians 4 v 28.**
>
> ❓ When, according to these verses, is enough wealth enough?
>
> ❓ How should a Christian's motivation differ from that of the man in **Ecclesiastes 4 v 8**? Should a Christian ever be in the same position as this man?

A miserable business

It is easy to mock, but much harder to get off the treadmill ourselves. Actually in many cases, we are working because we don't know how to stop doing it, or we are working because we don't like to think about what we'd *have* to think about if we stopped! No wonder the Preacher describes this slavery to work as a *"miserable* business". It is pointless twice over—meaningless as a purpose for life and producing unnecessary wealth.

> *time out*
>
> ❓ How wise in the light of scripture is the attitude to work and wealth in your church, your house-group or your home?
>
> ❓ How could you help each other to "break out of the mould" of the world on this?

> *pray thru'*
>
> Pray for wisdom to know how much work to do, for whom, and why.
>
> **Read Romans 12 v 1-2** and pray that in *your work* you will "not conform any longer to the pattern of this world".

Wisdom of companionship

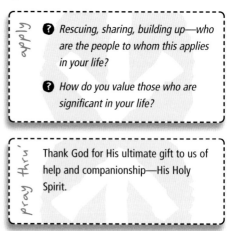

Reading: Ecclesiastes 4 v 9-12

*P*revious sections have dealt with the experiences of the oppressed suffering without a comforter, and the futility of the lonely workaholic. *Now the Preacher turns to one of God's blessings that can alleviate the bitterness of a life without meaning—companionship. Note that this is not about **using** people as the workaholic might; people always have value, even in our work situation.*

Two are better than one

▶ **Read Ecclesiastes 4 v 9-12**

❓ *What three examples does the Preacher give here of two being "better than one"?*

time out

❓ *What sort of "pairings" should we consider in the light of this passage? Are there enough "significant others" in your own life?*

❓ *In what way should Christians be uniquely privileged in this matter of companionship?*

The true value of a companion is that one can help the other out. The Preacher gives three practical examples of this: friends who help one another up when they fall, friends who lie together for warmth, and friends who defend one another against attack. Rescue from difficulties, sharing of resources, assistance with problems—as the Preacher says, such a three-stranded cord is not quickly broken!

The "cord of three strands" verse is often used in the address at a wedding, the third "strand" being interpreted as God in the relationship. But there is no reason why this should not also be true of siblings, colleagues, friends or companions of any sort.

Opposite opportunities

The armed forces have long recognised the importance of the "oppo", the opposite number who looks out for you in the same way you look out for them. In our individualistic culture, we need to listen to the observations of the Preacher. Two *are* better than one, and true companionship is far more beneficial than going solo.

▶ **Read Romans 15 v 1-6**

apply

❓ *Rescuing, sharing, building up—who are the people to whom this applies in your life?*

❓ *How do you value those who are significant in your life?*

pray thru'

Thank God for His ultimate gift to us of help and companionship—His Holy Spirit.

Preliminary findings

Reading: Ecclesiastes 4 v 13-16   **Sunday** 18 December

This first section of Ecclesiastes finishes with a proverbial story.

Old and wise?

Read Ecclesiastes 4 v 13 – 16

The "poor youth", in Old Testament understanding, would have little standing in the community; there is no comparison between him and the old king. But what if the king no longer listens to advice? Here, the youth is the one who people follow, and he will take over the king's position (v 15). The wise youth of humble origins gets a deservedly better public following than the old king who has become foolish (v 16a).

But, unfortunately, that is *not* the end of the matter, for the next generation turns its back on the very wisdom which has allowed them to prosper (v 16b).

And so, as the Preacher finally observes, even the goal of establishing a well-founded, prosperous society is, again, "chasing after the wind" (v 16). Indeed, a Solomon can be replaced by a Rehoboam...

Hearing what you want to hear...

After Solomon's death, Rehoboam wanted to be recognised as king by the northern tribes, but needed to take advice.

Read 1 Kings 12 v 1-16

❓ *From whom does Rehoboam seek advice?*

time out

❓ When faced with difficult decisions, do you know someone genuinely godly and wise whom you could ask for advice?

Our story so far...

At the end of this section of Ecclesiastes, examining the essential "meaninglessness" of human endeavour, we need to praise God for the critical mind of the Preacher, refusing to accept the simple answers people usually give for "what's it all about".

He is neither a pessimist nor a cynic, but is still determined to "dig deeper".

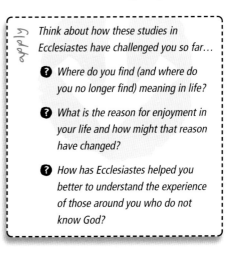

apply

Think about how these studies in Ecclesiastes have challenged you so far...

❓ Where do you find (and where do you no longer find) meaning in life?

❓ What is the reason for enjoyment in your life and how might that reason have changed?

❓ How has Ecclesiastes helped you better to understand the experience of those around you who do not know God?

Christmas: Certainty

Have you ever felt uncertain about whether the Christian faith really is true? Whether what you've heard about Christ can really be trusted?

If so, you've got something in common with most Christians: and with a first-century believer called Theophilus.

---

time out

❓ What kind of things make Christians doubt that the Gospels are true?

❓ Why might we sometimes want a section of a Gospel not really to be true?

❓ Are there any parts of the Gospel stories you find hard to believe?

▶ **Read Luke 1 v 1-4**

Why Luke wrote

Luke is writing to Theophilus (v 3). It's probable that he was an actual person, although, because that name means "lover of God", it's possible that Luke had a more general initial audience in mind.

❓ What's Luke's purpose for writing his book to Theophilus?

What Luke wrote

❓ Luke says others have drawn up "an account" (v 1). What phrase does he use to describe what their "accounts" are talking about?

Luke's carefully drawing a link between what his Gospel will say has happened,

and what the Old Testament had promised would happen. As we read his Gospel, we should expect to see the Old Testament promises that God had made being "fulfilled" on every page.

❓ How does Luke know about any of these things (v 2)?

❓ Why does it matter to Theophilus, and to us, that Luke knew these kind of people?

❓ What had Luke been doing as he prepared to write his Gospel (v 3)?

❓ Why does it matter to Theophilus, and to us, that Luke went about his work in this way?

To put it in 21st-century language, Luke was a historian. This is what historians do. They listen to the eye-witnesses, carefully investigate, interview, and check things out: and then write down what actually happened in an orderly, easily understandable way, so that people can know with "certainty" (v 4) what really happened.

---

apply

❓ How should these verses affect how we read the strange parts and the tough parts of Luke?

❓ Who do you know who you could tell about Luke 1 v 1-4 this Christmas, so that they might be challenged by the historical nature of what Luke writes?

Once in a lifetime

Ever had a once-in-a-lifetime experience *(apart from being born!)? Today we meet a man who did: and who found it was more terrifying, and more wonderful, than he could believe.*

A couple's pain

▶ **Read v Luke 1 v 5-7**

❓ *What are we told about Zechariah and his wife Elizabeth (v 5-6)?*

❓ *But despite his position and their godliness, what is missing from their lives (v 7)?*

A priest's privilege

▶ **Read verses 8-10**

Zechariah is here chosen to go into the Holy Place in the temple in Jerusalem; the area of the temple where God dwelled. He'll only do this once in his whole life of serving as a priest. It's a great moment for this old man, the high-light of his career.

God's plan

▶ **Read verses 11-17**

Zechariah gets more than he could possibly have imagined! When he goes into the Holy Place, an angel, a heavenly messenger, is standing there!

❓ *How does Zechariah (understandably) react (v 12)?*

❓ *What is the angel's message (v 13)?*

❓ *What do we learn about their son's:*
- *effect (v 14, 16)?*
- *relationship with God (v 15)?*
- *mission (v 17)?*

▶ **Read verses 18-22**

❓ *How does Zechariah react to the angel's words (v 18)?*

❓ *What is the angel's message to him (v 19-20)?*

Zechariah would have had plenty of time in the quietness of his head to realise that what God plans, happens: however unlikely or extraordinary it is.

A woman's pleasure

▶ **Read verses 23-25**

❓ *Why should what happens in verse 24 be no surprise to Elizabeth or Zechariah?*

❓ *How does Elizabeth respond (v 25)?*

> **time out**
> Luke's Gospel begins with God bringing life to a lifeless place: a living child in a barren womb. And it will end that way too: with a living man in a burial tomb. Truly, God is "the God who gives life to the dead" (Romans 4 v 17).

> **apply**
> ❓ *When God answers a prayer of yours, do you respond as Elizabeth did? Anything you need to praise and thank God for right now?*
>
> ❓ *How does this episode increase your faith in God's promises about the future?*

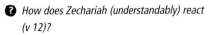

God sent the angel Gabriel

E lizabeth had experienced a miracle: but her son was only the support act. He was to "make ready a people prepared for the Lord" (v 17). God was about to step onto the stage, and in the most unexpected way…

pray thru'

It's said that "familiarity breeds contempt", and this can be the case with the Christmas story. Pray now that God would enable you to be struck by this story afresh, to see new truths in it, and to be moved to praise and love God more as you read about what He has done.

Troubled

▶ **Read Luke 1 v 26-29**

❓ What details does Luke tell us about Mary (v 26-27)?

❓ How did Mary react to the angel's words (v 28)? Why, do you think?

Visits from heaven are not comfortable experiences. Just as Zechariah found (v 12), and just as the shepherds would soon find (2 v 9), Mary doesn't find it easy to be caught up into God's plan.

Some Son!

▶ **Read verses 30-33**

❓ How does the angel describe the son Mary will carry?

Trusting

▶ **Read verses 34-38**

❓ How does Mary's response to Gabriel in verse 34 show more faith than Zechariah's (v 18)?

❓ What details does the angel give her (v 35)?

There's a glimpse here of the members of the Trinity working together to fulfil God's promises. The Father has sent Gabriel (v 26); the Spirit will cause Mary to fall pregnant; the one to be born will be "the Son of God" (v 35).

❓ Why would Elizabeth's experience (v 36-7) help Mary to trust the angel's words?

Mary was a young girl, probably aged about 13. In Israel, betrothal was binding, like marriage. A woman caught in adultery faced shame and possibly stoning.

❓ What is amazing about Mary's decision in verse 38?

Mary is a great example of faith in God's plan. Unlike Zechariah, she doesn't seem to doubt whether God's plan *will* happen, she simply wants to know *how* it will happen. And she turns her back on any prospect of a safe, secure life in order to be part what God's doing in the world.

apply

❓ How does what we see of God here encourage you today?

❓ How does Mary's attitude challenge you today?

Part of the plan

▶ Reading: Luke 1 v 39-55   **Thursday** 22 December

There were no ante-natal or birth classes in first-century Israel. But the elderly mum-to-be Elizabeth and the pregnant teenager Mary did get together as they waited for their babies to be born. And it's the first time we see the effect on people of knowing that God's Son has come to this world.

Elizabeth's words

▶ Read Luke 1 v 39-45

❓ How does Elizabeth describe Mary and her child (v 42)?

Here, it seems "blessed" = to know the satisfaction of being part of God's plan.

❓ Why does Elizabeth describe Mary in this way (v 43, 45)?

Notice that Elizabeth is "filled with the Holy Spirit" (v 41). Here we're seeing a godly, Spirit-filled response to the coming of God's Son.

A baby's leap

❓ How does Elizabeth's baby react to the arrival of Mary with Jesus (v 41)?

❓ Why did he react like this (v 44)?

John started his part in God's plan before he was even born! From the womb, he was pointing people to Jesus as the Lord and joy-giver.

Mary's song

▶ Read verses 46-55

Mary's song is essentially in three parts. She speaks of what God has done for her as an individual (v 46-49); how God acts in the world (v 50-53); and what God is doing for His people (v 54-55).

❓ How do these three parts each help us see what Jesus "the Lord" has come to do?

❓ Who is Mary's song all about?

❓ How is Mary a picture of what a "blessed" life looks like?

Mary never points to herself; she repeatedly points away from herself, towards God. And Elizabeth understands that Mary is "blessed ... among women" (v 42) because of "the child you will bear". Mary never sought nor encouraged praise of, or prayer to, herself. She encourages us to glorify and rejoice in the great God, who has broken into history in the person of her son.

---

apply

❓ Is your greatest satisfaction in life found in knowing that you're part of God's plan?

❓ Is your greatest joy in life found in knowing Jesus as your Lord?

Pray that today the centre of your life, and the motivation for your actions, would not be a desire for power (v 52), nor gaining wealth (v 53), but knowing and serving "God my Saviour" (v 47).

Choosing his words carefully

While Elizabeth and Mary were speaking and singing about God's goodness, Elizabeth's husband Zechariah was literally speechless (verse 20). But the time was coming for his words to return. What would he use them to do?

A strange name

Read Luke 1 v 56-66

? How are the events of verses 59-64 an "undoing" of what had happened to Zechariah in the temple (v 11-22)?

? What were the crowd expecting Zechariah to name his baby?

In naming his son John, the new father is showing that he's now fully signed up to God's plan. He would rather follow God's lead than tradition's, or society's. Where once there was doubt and disbelief, now there is a deep confidence and trust in the truth of God's word.

? What does a tongue loosed by trusting in God's word do (v 64)?

An amazing plan

Read verses 67-80

Zechariah's Spirit-directed praise outlines for us both what God is up to, and who He is doing it through.

? Pick out the phrases which tell us what God was doing in Zechariah's day.

? How is He doing this (the "horn" symbolises strength) (v 69)?

? In light of verses 31-32, who is being spoken of here?

time out
The "enemies" (v 74) Zechariah meant were probably the occupying Romans.

Read Luke 11 v 14-22.

? Which ultimate enemy did Jesus, the one "in the house of his servant David" (v 69), come to defeat?

And so Zechariah finished by prophesying a much greater consequence of God's plan than a simple political rescue (v 78-79). God has come to bring the light of life to those "in the shadow of death".

? What role will Zechariah's son, John, play in God's great plan (v 76-77)?

? What result would God's actions have for His people (v 74-75)?

apply
We've seen the right response to seeing God's plan of salvation unfold is to praise God (v 64), to serve God freely, and to live a holy life ie: become like Him (v 75).

? How can you do each of these things a little more today?

pray thru'
Choose a couple of phrases from Zechariah's wonderful song, and use them to praise "the Most High".

The time came

Most parents-to-be today pack an overnight bag and work out the quickest route to the hospital, to keep the great arrival as straightforward and stress-free as possible. The details of the Christmas story are so wellknown to us that it's easy to miss the traumatic nature of the greatest of all arrivals...

❓ *Imagine you knew nothing of the first Christmas. If Mary's baby is God's Christ, how and where might you expect Him to be born?*

▶ **Read Luke 2 v 1-7**

Anticlimax

❓ *What factors make this birth so difficult?*

❓ *Who attends this king's birth?*

❓ *What is hugely anticlimactic about the coming of "the Son of the Most High"?*

What remarkable humility of God! Not only was He willing to live among His creatures in His creation; He was prepared to be born in uncomfortable surroundings, without any pomp or ceremony; without anyone really noticing.

He doesn't only know what it is to be human; He knows what it is to be an unnoticed, average human.

But even in this anonymous arrival, God's hand is at work...

An emperor

❓ *Where is Jesus born (v 4-6)?*

❓ *Why are Joseph and Mary there (v 1-3)?*

What power! With a single stroke of a pen, this emperor can dictate the movement of countless people. Rome takes no account of pregnancy or inconvenience. Caesar speaks; Joseph and Mary move.

▶ **Read Micah 5 v 2-5a**

❓ *Who does God promise will come from Bethlehem (v 2)?*

❓ *What will he do, and what will life be like for his people (v 4-5a)?*

Lying behind the hand of Caesar ordering this tax census, a greater hand is arranging things according to a larger plan. A greater emperor even than the Roman one is in charge: and Jesus is born, not because of decisions made in Rome, but because of decisions made in heaven.

---

time out

Caesar Augustus encouraged his people to worship him as a god. By the time Luke wrote his historical Gospel, Christians were beginning to come under pressure to deny Jesus as Christ and bow down to the emperor.

Luke wants his readers to see that God's Christ isn't a normal king. He wasn't born like a king; He won't live like a king; He certainly won't die like one. But He's still God's promised King.

❓ *How would this passage have encouraged Christians in Luke's day?*

❓ *What in the world today are you tempted to worship as more powerful than Jesus?*

Joy to the world

Merry Christmas!

We've seen God turning expectations upside down in the way His Christ comes into the world. He chose an anonymous teenager as Jesus' mother; His Son's birth took place quietly and without ceremony; now the announcement of His arrival takes place on a hillside and to shepherds, whose job made them ritually unclean.

▶ **Read Luke 2 v 8-14**

An understandable reaction

❓ *What accompanied "the angel of the Lord" (v 9)?*

❓ *How did the shepherds respond (v 9)?*

It's not a surprising feeling—heaven is touching earth! And remember that these men know that they're unclean: certainly not ready to stand being in God's glory.

---

time out

Read Isaiah 6 v 1-7

❓ *How does Isaiah feel about being in the presence of God in His glory (v 5)?*

❓ *What does a seraph (an angel) say to him (v 6-7)?*

Meeting the perfect God should result in death for imperfect people—even for a prophet like Isaiah. But in Isaiah's case, it doesn't: an angel brings him a wonderful message of good news—that he has been saved from death.

And the shepherds were about to hear something wonderful too…

A wonderful message

❓ *What kind of message did the angel bring (v 10)?*

❓ *What four details did the angel give about the baby who "has been born to you" (v 11)?*

❓ *How does each detail show that this birth is "good news"?*

The gospel message prompts "great joy". **Joy** is the right response to God acting to fulfil His promises. John had "leaped for joy" in his mother's womb (1 v 44), and Mary had rejoiced (1 v 47). Now these seemingly randomly-chosen shepherds are also told to share the joy of knowing that the Ruler and Rescuer of the world has been born.

Ultimately, He's the one who saves people from death: who turns the prospect of meeting the glorious God from one of terror to one of joy: who brings peace between God and men who recognize His Christ and know Him as their Saviour (v 14). Happy Christmas!

---

apply

❓ *Have you paused from today's events to remember and appreciate the events of that day?*

❓ *Is your greatest joy today coming not from seeing family, eating food or being on holiday, but the fact that Christ the Lord has come?*

What they did next

▶ **Reading:** Luke 2 v 15-20

No one wanted to be a shepherd in first-century Israel. Their job was dull, dirty and dangerous; and the hours were very anti-social! But in this passage Luke presents them to us as people who respond in an exemplary way to the news that "Christ the Lord" has been born.

▶ **Read Luke 2 v 15-20**

Check the facts

As the angels disappeared, the shepherds' world went dark again. Imagine how they must have been feeling as they picked themselves off the ground and checked they were still alive!

❓ *What do they decide to do (v 15)?*

❓ *Is it that they don't believe the angels? Why do they go to Bethlehem?*

❓ *What do they find (v 16)?*

It's true! Right down to the detail of the baby "lying in a manger" (v 12).

❓ *How does the end of verse 20 sum up what the shepherds found in Bethlehem?*

---

time out

We've seen that Luke is writing as a historian (1 v 1-4). So he points us to cold, hard evidence, and to eyewitnesses.

The shepherds hear a remarkable claim: that God's Christ, God Himself ("the Lord"), has been born. But they don't simply believe it: they check the facts. They "see this thing that has happened" (v 15) with their own eyes.

▶ **Read Luke 24 v 9-12**

❓ *How do the apostles compare to the shepherds in how they listen to what God has done (v 11)?*

❓ *How is Peter similar to the shepherds (v 12)?*

Luke makes remarkable statements at the start and end of his Gospel: that God's Christ was born to a virgin, and that God's Christ rose from the dead.

❓ *Why does it matter greatly that people who weren't expecting these events SAW what had happened?*

Respond to the facts

❓ *What two things do the shepherds do once they've seen Jesus Christ (v 17, 20)?*

In some ways, the shepherds "returned" (v 20) to their normal lives. We don't hear from them again in Luke. But in a much deeper way, their lives would never be the same again. They'd met the Christ.

❓ *How does Mary react (v 19)?*

---

apply

❓ *We know Christ the Lord has come into the world. But how do we show that?*

❓ *Which do you most struggle with:*
  • *praising God in your everyday life?*
  • *telling others about Jesus?*
  • *setting the truth about Jesus deep in your heart and thinking about Him through your day?*

Focus on doing more of this today!

Giving Simeon space

▶ **Reading:** Luke 2 v 21-32

Simeon rarely gets a look-in at Christmas, even in churches (and never in Nativity plays!). But Luke devotes more space to him than to the shepherds or the angels. So it's right that we give him some time over the next couple of days.

But before we get to Simeon, Joseph and Mary need to get to Jerusalem…

A child of Israel

▶ **Read Luke 2 v 21-24**

❓ What do Joseph and Mary do:
- when Jesus is eight days old (v 21)?
- when Jesus is 40 days old, and Mary is able to enter the Jerusalem temple again (v 22-24)?

All firstborn children were dedicated to God; an animal was sacrificed in their place and they were to serve God all their lives. Jesus' earthly parents did all that members of Israel should do for their firstborn. He was, and lived as, a member of God's ancient chosen people.

Saving Israel and more

▶ **Read verses 25-32**

❓ What kind of man was Simeon (v 25)?

❓ What did he know (v 26)?

And he recognises, in the baby in Mary's arms, what he's been waiting all his life to see!

❓ What does Simeon see in this child (v 30)?

❓ How else does he describe him (v 32)? What do you think he means by these phrases?

In the coming of the Christ, God's glory came to Israel, to His ancient chosen people. And glory was offered to Israel; the opportunity to be at peace with God finally, eternally (2 v 14).

But Simeon says Jesus has come to do more than save Israel; He's come to reveal God to non-Jews, to the Gentiles. In Luke we'll find Jesus continually reaching out to those beyond "good Israel"; to Jews who've lost their way, and to Gentiles who have never known the way.

This would have been surprising to many Jews of Jesus' day. Surely God's Christ would want to spend time with, and be of help to, His people, and particularly His people who were obeying His rules?

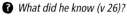

It's easy for us to miss the modern-day challenge of Simeon's words here.

Who are the people who live around us who we make no effort to reach with the news of Jesus the Christ? Are there "types" of people who you never see in your church, and who your church never deliberately seeks out with the gospel? How can we as Christians seem like rule-keepers who look down on rule-breakers?

❓ How does this challenge you as an individual, and as a member of your church?

As good as it gets

▶ **Reading:** Luke 2 v 33-39   **Wednesday** 28 December

L uke's Gospel begins with a rush of untainted good news. John is born to announce the arrival of the Christ: then Jesus Himself comes along. Elizabeth and Mary show faith: Zechariah learns to trust God's word. The shepherds meet God's King with joy and praise. Simeon knows he's seen what he's been waiting for: God's salvation wrapped up in a tiny bundle.

But Simeon knows something else, too—that it won't always be like this.

Falling

▶ **Read Luke 2 v 33-35**

❓ *What does Simeon say Mary's child will do (v 34-35a)?*

By no means all those who think of themselves as God's people will welcome God's Christ. And some surprising truths about people's inner relationship with God will be made clear.

---

time out

Read Luke 18 v 9-14.

❓ *Who falls, and who rises, in this parable?*

❓ *What attitudes of heart is Jesus comparing here?*

This played out many times throughout Jesus' ministry. Read **Luke 5 v 27-32** to see Jesus turning expectations on their head. He hadn't come for the "righteous" (those who thought they were good enough for God) but for "sinners" (those who knew they weren't).

Piercing

❓ *What does Simeon say will happen to Mary (2 v 35)?*

There are few things more painful than watching your child die. Mary would one day experience that pain (23 v 49). This is the first hint in Luke that the crib would lead to the cross; that the reaction of Elizabeth, of the shepherds, and of Simeon would not often be seen again.

Redeeming

❓ *Do Simeon's words in verses 34-35 suggest that Christ will succeed, or fail?*

▶ **Read verses 36-39**

Anna tells everyone she can find that this child is crucial for bringing about something.

❓ *What is it (v 38)?*

Simeon's and Anna's words set up a tension that will be resolved only at the end of this baby's life. He is the all-powerful Christ, come to redeem Jerusalem, to bring His people back to God; but He will have to be opposed by Jerusalem, and die just outside Jerusalem, to do that.

---

pray thru'

Thank Jesus the Christ that He came not just to rule, but to redeem, to rescue.

Ask Jesus to show you where the thoughts of your heart displease Him: any ways in which pride, self-righteousness, or disobedience are creeping in.

Father and son

W e're only told of one episode in the life of Jesus between His birth and the start of His ministry, aged about 30. Since today's passage is the only glimpse we have of His childhood, it's well worth examining it closely.

▶ **Read Luke 2 v 40-52**

Jesus and "my Father"

❓ *How do you think Joseph and Mary would have felt during verses 44-46?*

❓ *What emotions would you have had once you'd found this child?!*

❓ *What was Jesus busy doing while He was "lost" (v 46-47)?*

Unsurprisingly, Jesus' mother is pretty annoyed in verse 48!

❓ *What do you make of Jesus' response (v 49)?*

In verse 48, Mary talks to Jesus about "Your father", meaning Joseph. In verse 49, as He replies, Jesus says: "my Father", meaning God.

❓ *What is Jesus gently reminding Mary of here?*

❓ *Which relationship is most important to Jesus?*

❓ *Though that relationship was His priority, what did He not stop doing (v 51)?*

Us and our children

Of course, Jesus' childhood was unique. And so was His relationship with His Father, God in heaven.

But notice how He gently rebukes His mother for being annoyed that He wanted to spend more time in His Father's house, discussing eternal matters with human experts. He seems to be saying: "You should know my relationship with my Father God comes first. And you should be pleased that I put that first. I will obey you as your child; but knowing my Father is more important than anything else in my life."

So the challenge to those of us who are parents is: is that what we want for our children? Do we want them to know God as their Father more than anything, and do we want them to put their relationship with Him first?

Are we more pleased by our children's grades, jobs, sporting achievements or good manners than we are by their desire to read their Bibles, pray to God, and meet with His people in church?

> *apply*
>
> ❓ *If you are a parent, do you need to encourage your children to put knowing their heavenly Father first by:*
> - *changing the family routine?*
> - *changing what you talk to them about?*
> - *changing what things you show them you're passionate about?*
>
> ❓ *Parent or not, what changes could you resolve to make next year so that YOU put knowing and growing in your relationship with God before everything else?*

Personal praise

▶ **Reading:** Psalm 146   **Friday** 30 December

*T*he last five songs in the psalter are entirely devoted to praising God. There's no asking for help, no confession, depression or confusion. And surely this is where we should all end up. Following Jesus Christ, and living to the glory of God, is often confusing, difficult and draining, but in the end, it is our duty and our joy to praise our Maker and Saviour, and to trust Him for the parts where life is a struggle.

▶ **Read Psalm 146**

Who needs help?

▶ **Read v 1-2**

❓ *Who is he talking to in v 1?*

❓ *What is he urging himself to do?*

❓ *Why do you think he needs to talk to himself like this?*

> *apply*
>
> Other psalms in this last section urge us to encourage each other to praise God. Here, the writer is talking to himself! The first sign of madness in the Christian life is when we *stop* talking to ourselves! Our hearts, we know, are desperately wicked. And our temptation is to give in to self-pity when our lives are hard. So we need to keep preaching to ourselves, urging our cold hearts to give God due credit for all that is ours in Christ.
>
> ❓ *What sermon do you need to preach to yourself today?*

Who not to praise

▶ **Read v 3-4**

❓ *Find three reasons why it's just plain stupid to praise mere humans.*

❓ *How is God the exact opposite of all this?*

> *time out*
>
> ❓ *How do we thank people properly for things they have done, for us, or in church, for example, and yet give the glory where it belongs—to God?*

Who to praise

▶ **Read v 5-10**

Notice that it's not just *any* Creator God that we need to praise. The God of the Bible is the God who made everything (v 6), but who also cares passionately about people (v 7-9), and about justice (v 7a, 9c). Praising "the unknown God" is just not good enough. Our intelligent worship must be given to the LORD, who reveals Himself in Jesus Christ.

> *pray thru'*
>
> **Read v 5-10 again**, and think how the Lord Jesus fulfils each point through His life, death and resurrection.
>
> Now preach these truths to yourself (v 1), and give voice to your praise. Saying words of praise to God is just the start. To praise God truly is to become like Him in how we feel, what we do, what we want for others… Pray that your life will be like this in the coming year.

At a word

"*Isn't He great?*" Praising God is more than simply singing hymns loudly and with passion. One way we can think of it is that we are **advertising** *God's character and benefits to other people. In this psalm, we hear the people of God talking to one another about their great King, Creator and Provider.*

▶ Read Psalm 147

Good... pleasant... fitting

▶ Read v 1

Sometimes we need to stir ourselves to praise God—by reminding ourselves of what He has done for us. But notice that singing praises should be something that we delight in, and enjoy! Our praises should bring us pleasure... remember that as you stand to sing hymn no. 353!

The God who cares

▶ Read v 2-6

As we sing to each other, we should also remind ourselves *who we really are*, and the reason for which we have been brought together:

Gathered exiles—deservedly banished from the garden, and undeservingly, but miraculously, brought back into it.

Wounded and broken—but by His mercy and grace, our hearts have been restored, and our wounds bound up. As you sit in church next time, look around, and as you see those whom God has been specially gracious to, pause to give thanks for them—and praise to their God and yours.

Being built up—God is doing a work in the world—building His people.

❓ *Which of these verses means most to you? Why?*

The God who provides

▶ Read v 7-11

❓ *What does God love to do (v 8-9)?*

There is the special grace that God works for His people through the gospel. But God's mercy extends to all mankind in the reliability of the seasons, His provision of food for the world, and the wealth of riches He has given us in human love, in art and nature. We may be impressed by the strength of men and animals (v 10)...

❓ *...but what does God truly value (v 11)?*

The God who speaks

▶ Read v 12-20

The elements are God's to command by His word for blessing to all mankind—but also for the judgment of His enemies and the reproof of His people (v 15-18).

❓ *What has God done for His people— the old and new Israel, His church?*

> apply
>
> Think about the reality of verses 13, 14, 19 and 20 for you, and then obey the command of v 12!

Quench your thirst!

Trying to live the Christian life without spending regular time reading God's word is like trying to cross the desert without water. That's why our daily Bible-reading resources aim to bring you the refreshment of God's truth every day. Don't miss out on your daily Bible readings with *Explore*. Order a subscription for a whole year.

Visit your friendly neighbourhood website for further details

N AMERICA:
www.thegoodbook.com
t (toll free): 866 244 2165
e: sales@thegoodbook.com

UK & EUROPE:
www.thegoodbook.co.uk
t: 0333 123 0880
e: admin@thegoodbook.co.uk

SOUTH AFRICA:
www.christianbooks.co.za
t: (021) 674 6931/2
e: nick@christianbooks.co.za

AUSTRALIA:
www.thegoodbook.com.au
t: (02) 6100 4211
e: admin@www.thegoodbook.com.au

NEW ZEALAND:
www.thegoodbook.co.nz
t: (+64) 3 343 1990

Introduce a friend to Explore

Why not encourage a friend to start using *Explore* by giving them a copy of *Time with God*, our introductory issue with 30 days of readings?
Details over the page...

Time with God

In the next issue

- ▶ 2 Corinthians
- ▶ Ecclesiastes
- ▶ Luke
- ▶ 2 Timothy
- ▶ Psalms

Don't miss your copy. Contact your local Christian bookshop or church agent, or go to one of the websites listed below, to get the next issue.

Contact us...

UK & EUROPE
www.thegoodbook.co.uk
t: 0845 225 0880
e: admin@thegoodbook.co.uk

AUSTRALIA
www.thegoodbook.com.au
t: (02) 6100 4211
e: admin@www.thegoodbook.com.au

N AMERICA
www.thegoodbook.com
t (toll free): 866 244 2165
e: sales@thegoodbook.com

NEW ZEALAND
www.thegoodbook.co.nz
t: (+64) 3 343 1990

SOUTH AFRICA
www.christianbooks.co.za
t: (021) 674 6931/2

Introduce a friend to Explore!

If you're enjoying using *Explore*, why not introduce a friend? Visit your local website to order our introductory issue: *Time with God*.

Contributors

Graham Beynon (Daniel) was minister at Avenue Community Church, Leicester, UK and is currently studying in Cambridge.

John Richardson (Ecclesiastes) is a minister in Elsenham and Ugley in Essex, UK.

Alison Cripps (Ecclesiastes) is an editor for The Good Book Company.

Carl Laferton (Luke, 1 Timothy) works at The Good Book Company.

Tim Thornborough (Psalms) works at The Good Book Company.

Mark Wallace (1 Thessalonians) is a curate at All Saints Trull, Taunton, UK.

Editor: Tim Thornborough.

Production team: Nicole Carter, Carl Laferton, Alison Mitchell, Anne Woodcock.

Cover design: André Parker.